A Sourcebook about Sunday

A Sourcebook about Sunday

A Sourcebook about Sunday

Compiled by

Paul F. Ford

Mary Ellen Hynes

J. Michael Thompson

Art by

Julie Lonneman

LITURGY
TRAINING
PUBLICATIONS

Acknowledgments

We are grateful to the many authors and publishers who have given permission to include their work. Every effort has been made to determine the ownership of all texts and to make proper arrangements for their use. Any oversight that may have occurred, if brought to our attention, will gladly be corrected in future editions.

We are also grateful to those who suggested material: Robert Baker, Margaret Brennan, Sister Jeanne Cropo, Todd Johnson, Maria Leonard, Peter Mazar, Jim McGuinness, Nathan Mitchell, Gail Ramshaw, Virginia Sloyan, and Kathleen Sullivan Stewart.

Acknowledgments will be found in the endnotes. Permission to reprint any texts in this book must be obtained from the copyright owners.

Scripture quotations, unless otherwise indicated, are from the *New Revised Standard Version* of the Bible, copyright © 1989 by the Division of Christian Education of the National Council of the Churches of Christ in the USA. Used by permission. All rights reserved.

This book was edited by Lorie Simmons. Carol Mycio was the production editor. The design is by Anna Manhart, and the type-setting was done by Jim Mellody-Pizzato and Kari Nicholls in Optima. The art on pages 1, 9, 25, 33, 44, 62, 154, and 165 is from clipart.com. Andrea McClure secured the permissions. The format for the SOURCEBOOK series was designed by Michael Tapia.

A SOURCEBOOK ABOUT SUNDAY © 2005 Archdiocese of Chicago: Liturgy Training Publications, 1800 North Hermitage Avenue, Chicago IL 60622-1101; 1-800-933-1800, fax 1-800-933-7094, e-mail orders@ltp.org. All rights reserved. See our website at www.ltp.org.

Printed in the United States of America.

Library of Congress Control Number: 2005924152

ISBN 1-56854-255-0

SUNSB

Contents

Introduction

Special Sunday observances are rare in most households today, but as the witnesses on these pages testify, celebrating the Lord's Day and honoring the Sabbath have been central spiritual practices in the Christian and Jewish traditions. In this Year of the Eucharist, 2004–2005, Pope John Paul II has invited us to return to a deeper experience of Sunday. You will find his Apostolic Letter *Dies Domini, On Keeping the Lord's Day Holy,* quoted frequently in this book.

Undergirding all aspects of Sunday and Sabbath explored in *Sourcebook about Sunday* is the history of Sabbath-keeping within the larger context of salvation history. In obedience to the third commandment, the people of ancient Israel kept the Sabbath on the seventh day, Saturday, as modern Jews continue to do. As we re-immerse ourselves in the holiness of Sunday, Jewish understandings of Shabbat continue to offer insights, which you will find here. Early Christians transferred their holy pause from Saturday to Sunday, adding to the commandment their thundering new awareness of the Paschal Mystery—Christ's death, and the Resurrection on the first day of the week. Quoting a fourth-century homily, the Holy Father reminds us in *Dies Domini* that because Sunday is the day of Christ's Resurrection, " 'the Lord's Day' is 'the lord of days.' "

This collection of excerpts follows the Friday through Monday cycle that we live every week, setting a banquet table with texts from many centuries and genres. It recalls the liturgical, social, and familial ways that people have observed these days with deep awareness of God's saving love for us.

If read straight through, the book could serve as a Friday through Monday retreat, furnishing material for reflection on each day. It is also intended to catalyze insights and provide texts for those preparing programs about the Lord's Day. Enter this temporal panorama at any point and see what resonates, encourages, or confronts you.

This book has been shaped by the vision and expertise of several editors and many contributors. Gabe Huck had already given much thought to the riches of full celebrations of the Lord's Day when he asked Paul Ford and J. Michael Thompson to gather material for the project. Some time later he asked me to build on their foundation and LTP put out a call to many literary-minded colleagues around the country to suggest pieces for the book. The late Peter Mazar gave advice and encouragement.

Few will read this book without the startling recognition that Sunday is a handsome but forgotten inheritance waiting to be claimed. "Without Sunday we cannot be, we cannot live." This is how early fourth-century North African Christians expressed their feelings about Sunday as they faced torture and death for participating in the Sunday liturgy. What did they experience that was so vital? If we do not keep Sunday holy, are we not starving ourselves of spiritual nourishment? This collection will demonstrate how deep is our need for Sunday, how long we have neglected it, and how lavish are the possibilities for fulfillment. May it provide intriguing perspectives on Sabbath-keeping and entice you into a fuller observance of the Lord's Day.

Mary Ellen Hynes

SOON enough, Jesus rests in death. Like a seed planted in fertile ground, he must die to bear fruit. *Unless a grain of wheat falls into the earth and dies, it remains alone; but if it dies, it bears much fruit.* And so Jesus dies, and lies dormant for three days. Without this dormancy, the resurrection of new life would be impossible.

If God raised Jesus in three days, surely he could have been raised in two, or one, or even been made invincible. So why sentence him to death for three days? Because everything, even the anointed of God, must rest, even in death.

Unless the grain falls into the earth and dies, there will be no harvest. These three days are the necessary dormancy of a Sabbath, an emptiness in which Jesus may be reborn, and take on a new form. All form is either arising or falling away. And between falling away and arising again, there is an inevitable dormancy, . . . the emptiness of God.

Wayne Muller
Twentieth century

THE resurrection of Jesus is the fundamental event upon which Christian faith rests (cf. 1 Corinthians 15:14). It is an astonishing reality, fully grasped in the light of faith, yet historically attested to by those who were privileged to see the Risen Lord. It is a wondrous event which is not only absolutely unique in human history, but which lies *at the very heart of the mystery of time.* In fact, "all time belongs to [Christ] and all the ages," as the evocative liturgy of the Easter Vigil recalls in preparing the paschal candle. Therefore, in commemorating the day of Christ's resurrection not just once a year but every Sunday, the church seeks to indicate to every generation the true fulcrum of history, to which the mystery of the world's origin and its final destiny leads.

Pope John Paul II
Twentieth century

Christ yesterday and today
the beginning and the end
Alpha
and Omega
all time belongs to him
and all the ages
to him be glory and power
through every age for ever.

*Roman rite,
Preparation of the
Candle, Easter Vigil*

AT the source of our celebrations is an energy of the Holy Spirit from which we must constantly drink, and this energy is the new time inaugurated by the resurrection. It is this time that enters into our days, weeks, and years, until our old time is saturated with it and the mortal veil that covers our old time is at last rent. But even now, "today," we can participate in this new time.

*Jean Corbon
Twentieth century*

SABBATH after sabbath, through Friday fasts and Sunday feasts, Christians are formed in the mystery of the death, rest and resurrection of the Lord. This paschal mystery is the mystery of the week, of the passage of time from sabbath into eternal sabbath, from first day into eighth day. God has offered the week as a gift, first formed in the creation of the world. The gift is to count seven days and then to find that the beginning is the end.

When time has made weeks into a gentle routine, a way of life, gradually they will be perceived not as a circle, recurring round after round. Gradually they will be known for what they are—a spiral staircase, Jacob's ladder ascending into heaven.

*Peter Mazar
Twentieth century*

days of the Lord, and even like the day of the Pasch, because every day the heavenly Lamb immolates Himself for them and is eaten by them."

Abbé Durand
Nineteenth century

THE sabbath plays a very important role in the festal year. It is the end and crown of the seven-day week and may be called the primordial feast day of the Jewish people: a day of rest but also of openness to Yahweh and his word. Its establishment as binding upon Israel must be traced back at least to the time of the exile. . . .

The Jewish sabbath was not only a day of rest from work, on which the people sought to imitate "the repose of God" after his work of six days and to approach the Lord. It was also a day for "a holy convocation" and an "appointed feast of the Lord" (Leviticus 23:3 and 2). In the temple at Jerusalem special sabbath sacrifices were offered. (cf. Numbers 28:9 –10). During the exile, when there was no temple, and later in places outside Jerusalem the Jewish communities met for a liturgy consisting of prayers and readings. The place of assembly was the synagogue which, in the opinion of many scholars, came into existence soon after the exile wherever a reasonably large number of Jews had settled. At these assemblies there were, among other things, readings from the Law and the prophets, as well as explanations of them.

Adolph Adam
Twentieth century

NEHEMIAH relates in the biblical book that bears his name that, upon his return to Palestine, he was shocked to see the widespread desecration of the holy day. On the Sabbath people labored in the fields, gathered the harvests, bought and sold publicly. Nehemiah rebuked the nobles of Judah and ordered the gates of Jerusalem closed during the Sabbath (Nehemiah 13:15–22). His vigorous efforts finally led to the establishment of the Sabbath as a day of univer-sal rest among the Jews of Palestine.

The religious revival initiated by Ezra and Nehemiah and deepened by their disciples, the *Sopherim* (Scribes), ultimately made Sabbath observance a matter of universal concern. There developed a complicated code of restrictions calculated to insure complete rest on the Sabbath. These restrictions were meant to safeguard and preserve the spirit of the Sabbath, in the same manner as the shell protects the kernel. The *Sopherim* were remarkably successful in their efforts, for the concept of the Sabbath as a day of delightful rest and as a day of spiritual and intellectual edification reached its fullest development during their era. . . .

By the beginning of the Common Era, the Sabbath, as we know it, had been almost fully developed both in its theory and practice.

Abraham Millgram
Twentienth century

THE Christian celebration of the first day began as early as the week following on the resurrection of Christ: "Eight days later, his disciples were again in the house. . . . Jesus came and stood among them, and said, 'Peace be with you.' Then he said to Thomas, 'Put your finger here, and see my hands; and put out your hand, and place it in my side; do not be faithless, but believing'" (John 20:26–27).

The apostolic generation immediately grasped the importance of the first day, connected as it was with the memory and presence of the crucified and risen Jesus. . . . The Acts of the Apostles gives us a description of the assembly at Troas in which Paul was the central figure: "On the first day of the week . . . we were gathered together to break bread" (Acts 20:7–12). The gathering took place at night, on the third story of a Christian's home; it included a lengthy sermon by Paul and the breaking of bread. . . .

Sunday was so important in the life of the Church that testimonies to its celebration have survived in abundance. It is very likely, of course, that the Jerusalem community had to be satisfied with adding the Sunday Eucharistic assembly to the sabbath observance. But by about the end of the first century the separation of the two was complete. . . .

The Acts of the Martyrs of Abitina show that when the period of persecution was ending the Church had already fully grasped the sacramental reality of Sunday, a day which brought intense joy to the Christian people even in the midst of the most severe trials. The advent of peace now meant that even the laws of the empire paid homage to Sunday. Faithful to his intention of promoting simultaneously the cult of the sun and the cult of Christ, Constantine was glad to honor both the sun-god and Christ by making a holiday of the day that was at once the day of the sun and the day of Kyrios Christ. . . .

On the eve of the Council of Nicaea, then, the Christian Sunday was a day of liturgical assembly at which the Word of God was proclaimed and the Eucharist was celebrated; it was a day of festivity that was to find expression in the laying aside of everyday tasks.

P. Jounel
Twentieth century

I N Abitina, a city of proconsular Africa, Saturninus, a Christian priest, was celebrating the holy mysteries one Sunday [in the early fourth century] when the magistrates with a troop of soldiers broke in upon them and seized forty-nine men and women. Among them were the priest Saturninus with his four children, namely, Saturninus the younger and Felix, who were both lectors, Mary, who had consecrated herself to God, and Hilarion, a little boy. Besides these the names are recorded of Dativus and another Felix, who were senators, Thelica, Emeritus, Ampelius, Rogatian and Victoria. Dativus and Saturninus with his children headed the procession of captives who were led before the magistrates. When questioned they confessed their faith so resolutely that the very judges applauded their courage. . . . The prisoners taken at Abitina were shackled and sent to Carthage, the residence of the proconsul, and during their journey they sang hymns and psalms to God, praising His name and rendering Him thanks.

The proconsul first examined the senator Dativus, asking him who and what he was and whether he had attended the assembly of the Christians. He replied that he was a Christian and worshipped with Christians. The proconsul asked who presided at these meetings and in whose house the assemblies took place, but, without waiting for an answer, ordered that Dativus should be racked to make him confess. Thelica when questioned as to their ringleader replied at once, "The holy priest Saturninus and all of us with him." Emeritus boldly acknowledged that the assemblies took place in his house, and in reference to the Holy Scriptures said to be kept there replied that he kept them in his heart. In spite of torture they one and all made profession that they were Christians and that they had been present on Sundays at the "collects," that is to say, the celebration of the liturgy. Women were as brave as men in enduring suffering and in proclaiming Christ. . . .

It appears that they all died in prison, either from the length of their confinement or from torture and the hardships they had undergone.

Butler's Lives
of the Saints

I T was Jerome in his Vulgate who gave the Latin-speaking world the term *opus servile.* For centuries Christians have argued whether the motive for which a work was done or its intrinsic nature was the chief determinant of servile work, the latter tradition coming to prevail. . . .

The concept was originally of great social benefit in the relief it provided to serfs in feudal organization. It kept this advantage throughout the industrial revolution with the new forms of human servitude introduced by that age. Still, in the lifetimes of most of those now living the notion had degenerated into arguments about sewing, and whether the white-collar class did not welcome a little servile work on Sunday as an alternative to the monotony of its liberal weekday employments.

Gerard S. Sloyan
Twentieth century

W HILE "servile work" was forbidden to Catholics on Sundays and holy days, the New England Puritan legacy broadened the Roman Catholic definition of opus servile to exclude even the most innocent divertissements on the Lord's Day. . . .

Until the middle of the nineteenth century, American Catholicism, like its original source (English Catholicism), knew a liturgical piety and spirituality which shaped the average Catholic's understanding of the nature and meaning of Sunday. . . . The shift in meaning seems to have come about with the introduction of a Counter-Reformation spirituality when European immigration was on the rise. Coupled with a new-found "Americanism," one of the principal pillars of which was a fundamental sabbatarianism, "Catholic Sunday in America" came to be a spiritual expression several times removed from true liturgical piety, ultimately necessitating . . . the sweeping reforms advocated by the American liturgical movement.

John Gurrieri
Twentieth century

IF you refrain from trampling the sabbath,
   from pursuing your own interests on my holy day;
if you call the sabbath a delight
   and the holy day of the LORD honorable;
if you honor it, not going your own ways,
   serving your own interests, or pursuing your own affairs,
then you shall take delight in the LORD,
   and I will make you ride upon the heights of the earth;
I will feed you with the heritage of your ancestor Jacob,
   for the mouth of the LORD has spoken.

Isaiah 58:13–14

REMEMBER the sabbath day, and keep it holy. Six days you shall labor and do all your work. But the seventh day is a sabbath to the LORD your God; you shall not do any work—you, your son or your daughter, your male or female slave, your livestock, or the alien resident in your towns. For in six days the LORD made heaven and earth, the sea, and all that is in them, but rested the seventh day; therefore the LORD blessed the sabbath day and consecrated it.

Exodus 20:8–11

THE first redaction of the Decalogue [Exodus 20:8–11] stresses rest from work on the sabbath (the word "sabbath" is probably from the Hebrew *shabbat,* "to leave off, to rest"). It connects the sabbath closely with God's resting after the six days of his work of creation. . . .

Other passages of the Old Testament emphasize the social and economic function of the sabbath: "that your manservant and your maidservant may rest as well as you" (Deuteronomy 5:14); "Six days you shall do your work, but on the seventh you shall rest; that your ox and your ass may have rest, and the son of your bondmaid, and the alien, may be refreshed" (Exodus 23:12). The sabbath is also to be regarded as a commemoration of the liberation from slavery in Egypt and as an obligatory sign of the covenant: "You shall remember that you were a servant in the land of Egypt, and the Lord your God brought you out thence with a mighty hand and an outstretched arm; therefore the Lord your God commanded you to keep the sabbath day" (Deuteronomy 5:15). The people of Israel are to keep the sabbath, observing it "throughout their generations, as a perpetual covenant. It is a sign for ever between me and the people of Israel" (Exodus 31:16–17).

Adolf Adam
Twentieth century

OBSERVE the sabbath day and keep it holy, as the LORD your God commanded you. Six days you shall labor and do all your work. But the seventh day is a sabbath to the LORD your God; you shall not do any work—you, or your son or your daughter, or your male or female slave, or your ox or your donkey, or any of your livestock, or the resident alien in your towns, so that your male and female slave may rest as well as you. Remember that you were a slave in the land of Egypt, and the LORD your God brought you out from there with a mighty hand and an outstretched arm; therefore the LORD your God commanded you to keep the sabbath day.

Deuteronomy 5:12–15

THE Sabbath precept, which in the first covenant prepares for the Sunday of the new and eternal covenant, is therefore rooted in the depths of God's plan. This is why, unlike many other precepts, it is set not within the context of strictly cultic stipulations but within the Decalogue, the "ten words" that represent the very pillars of the moral life inscribed on the human heart. In setting this commandment within the context of the basic structure of ethics, Israel and then the church declare that they consider it not just a matter of community religious discipline but *a defining and indelible expression of our relationship with God,* announced and expounded by biblical revelation. This is the perspective within which Christians need to rediscover this precept today. Although the precept may merge naturally with the human need for rest, it is faith alone which gives access to its deeper meaning and ensures that it will not become banal and trivialized.

Pope John Paul II
Twentieth century

THE third commandment, to keep holy the Sabbath, can be understood in its deeper, symbolic sense only within the context of the concerns expressed in the first two commandments. There it was a matter of violating the mystery of God through superstition and magic; here it is a question of violating the mystery of God's creation by attempting to dominate and manage it in a way that eliminates or endangers its essential mystery. . . .

Ideally, labor will always be a reflection of God's activity in creation, bringing order out of chaos and developing the immense resources of a world-becoming. But it may also be used, like idols and magic, to control and manage creation in a way that ignores and rejects God's presence in it and God's freedom to act in and through it. Labor or work can therefore be a device for eliminating mystery and rejecting God. For to reject God's mystery in creation is to reject it everywhere, even in God. It is another form of idolatry. . . .

Idolatry means to treat God as a power to be manipulated rather than as a person to be loved and trusted. And to violate the Sabbath is to treat God's creation, and especially God's people, as if they were puppets to be managed and controlled rather than persons to be loved and trusted. The commandments that follow the Sabbath precept in the decalogue are all concerned with respect, care and love for the subtle, mysterious, vulnerable and personal aspects of the world. Aged parents must receive tender care, fragile life must be nurtured and preserved, delicate love must be protected, possession by violence is condemned, fragile truth must be handled carefully, there is no place for the corrosive and disruptive influence of jealousy. Every one of these last seven commandments is a rejection of violence, domination and control and a call for tenderness, gentleness, and respect. In a word, Israel is commanded by God to be sensitive to and to care for and to rejoice in all that is personal in life. For the personal dimension of life is that habitat of mystery and freedom which is the hidden divine presence at the heart of being.

Demetrius Dumm
Twentieth century

THE Sabbath commandment is the longest and in some ways the most puzzling. Unlike any of the others, it takes quite different forms in the two passages where the Ten Commandments appear. Both versions require the same behavior—work on six days, rest on one—but each gives a different reason. What is wonderful is that each reason arises from a fundamental truth about God's relationship to humanity.

The Exodus commandment to "remember" the Sabbath day is grounded in the story of creation. The human pattern of six days of work and one of rest follows God's pattern as Creator; God's people are to rest on one day because God did. In both work and rest, human beings are in the image of God. At the same time, they are not God but God's creatures, who must honor God by obeying this commandment.

In Deuteronomy, the commandment to "observe" the Sabbath day is tied to the experience of a people newly released from bondage. Slaves cannot take a day off; free people can. When they stop work every seventh day, the people will remember that the Lord brought them out of slavery, and they will see to it that no one within their own dominion, not even animals, will work without respite.

Sabbath rest is a recurring testimony against the drudgery of slavery.

Together, these two renderings of the Sabbath commandment summarize the most fundamental stories and beliefs of the Hebrew Scriptures: creation and exodus, humanity in God's image and a people liberated from captivity. One emphasizes holiness, the other social justice. Sabbath crystallizes the Torah's portrait of who God is and what human beings are most fully meant to be.

Dorothy C. Bass
Twentieth century

ALL concepts of melakhah [work] stem from the original thirty-nine forbidden acts.

As an example of how these melakhot were later interpreted, the prohibition against reaping came to include a prohibition against any severing of a natural growing plant from its place of growth; accordingly, picking flowers, breaking tree branches, plucking up grass all came to be forbidden.

. . . Shabbat itself is the testimony that God is the Supreme Creator of heaven and earth. Our lives revolve around mastering our world—controlling God's creation. The more we try to control, the more we are in danger of forgetting just where we fit into the world. We too are dependent on God. We are beloved by Him, and share that love on the day of rest. Anyone who has ever tasted Shabbat knows the relief of laying down the burden for a while. . . .

The prohibition against melakhah, then, means refraining from interfering in the physical world. We let the physical world rest for a while, and it lets us rest for a while.

The Jewish Catalog
Twentieth century

So God blessed the seventh day and hallowed it, because on it God rested from all the work that he had done in creation.

Genesis 2:3

ONE of the most distinguished words in the Bible is the word *qadosh,* holy; a word which more than any other is representative of the mystery and majesty of the divine. Now what was the first holy object in the history of the world? Was it a mountain? Was it an altar?

It is, indeed, a unique occasion at which the distinguished word *qadosh* is used for the first time: in the Book of Genesis at the end of the story of creation. How extremely significant is the fact that it is applied to time: "And God blessed the seventh *day* and made it *holy.*"

There is no reference in the record of creation to any object in space that would be endowed with the quality of holiness.

Abraham Joshua Heschel
Twentieth century

IN our biblical tradition, the Sabbath as a holy day symbolized who we believe ourselves to be: a free people, liberated by the Lord. Sabbath-keeping, as the commandment shows, was a way to take that freedom from a matter of history to a matter of present delight: not only did freedom happen a long time ago for our ancestors, it happens in our lives right now. If it was a radical thought those thousands of years ago to declare independence one day in seven, it is nearly unthinkable today. The work week may be down to five or even four days, but all seven days and nights aren't enough for most of us to finish our agendas. Sabbath allowed one day in seven to be a free people. There are, of course, all kinds of slaveries. Doing the Sabbath can give us a fighting chance against all of them. . . .

Rest, then as now, is a radical activity which challenges the prevailing view of work and leisure. To observe the command is to keep alive what the liberation was all about, what the liberating God is all about. The Sabbath observed breaks routine, and that is the root of all possibilities.

Gabe Huck
Twentieth century

W HAT is meant by rest, *menuchah* in Hebrew, had a long history of development. The basic principle is found in Exodus 31:14, the commandment to abstain from any kind of productive activity. Specific prohibitions were eventually classified and elaborated by rabbinical tradition into thirty-nine categories, derived symbolically from the kinds of work involved in building the Temple. The principle involved in deciding what is work here is not so much the physical nature of an activity, but its *purpose.* If its intent signifies human power over nature, if it shows human mastery of the world by the purposeful and constructive exercise of intelligence and skill, then it is *meluchah,* work, which violates the restful intent of sabbath time to recognize our dependence on God as ultimate Creator-Sustainer. Here the sabbath is for God's sake, a day to be kept holy accordingly.

The story about the Israelites who gathered manna in Exodus 16:17–30 points to the *hubris* of those who continued to try and gather manna on the sabbath, despite having been given a double measure of food by God on the day of preparation that would last them through the sabbath, and despite the divine command to rest on that day. The story says that these overzealous workers found no manna. The sabbath is for rest, in which work finds its culmination.

Tilden Edwards
Twentieth century

T O be sure, the Mishnah does offer a generalized list of forbidden activities, which is the closest thing it has to a definition of forbidden labor.

The main categories of labor are forty less one: sowing, plowing, reaping, binding sheaves, threshing, winnowing, sorting, grinding, sifting, kneading, baking; shearing wool, washing it, beating it, dyeing it, spinning, weaving, making two loops, weaving two threads, separating in order to sew two stitches; trapping a deer, slaughtering it, skinning it, salting it, curing its hide, scraping it, cutting it up, writing two letters, erasing in order to write two letters; building, tearing down, putting out a fire, kindling a fire, striking with a hammer, taking anything from one domain into another. These are the main categories of labor, forty less one.

Food, clothing, and shelter are universal necessities of life, as every schoolchild learns, but this list is distinctive for the other category it includes, writing. The only writing the authors of this list could possibly have considered a necessity of life is the writing of the Torah. If the writing of the Torah must be done before the Sabbath, however, then the Sabbath must be a day for the study of the Torah thus prepared.

Robert Goldenberg
Twentieth century

GOD made the world in six days and rested on the seventh day. In other words, there is a rhythm at the back of things, and in the beginning and nature of the universe; and there must be something of the same kind in the social and secular manifestations of the world. Men are not happy if things always *look* the same; it is recognized in practice in the common medical case for what is called "a change.". . .

There is something in the very light and air of a world in which most people are not working, or not working as much or in the same way as usual, which satisfied the subconscious craving for crisis and fulfilment. If men have nothing but an endless series of days which look alike, it would matter little whether they were days of leisure or labour. They would not give that particular sense of something achieved, or, at least, of something measured; of the image of God resting on the seventh day. It is a psychological fact that such monotony would take on a character as of mathematical insanity. It would be like the endless corridors of a nightmare. Men have always known this by instinct.

G. K. Chesterton
Twentieth century

WHERE I come from we say that rhythm is the soul of life because the whole universe revolves around rhythm; and when we get out of rhythm, that's when we get into trouble.

Babatunde Olatunji
Twentieth century

We have familiar experience of the order, the constancy, the perpetual renovation of the material world which surrounds us. Frail and transitory as is every part of it, restless and migratory as are its elements, never-ceasing as are its changes, still it abides. It is bound together by a law of permanence, it is set up in unity; and, though it is ever dying, it is ever coming to life again. Dissolution does but give birth to fresh modes of organization, and one death is the parent of a thousand lives. Each hour, as it comes, is but a testimony, how fleeting, yet how secure, how certain is the great whole. It is like an image on the waters, which is ever the same, though the waters ever flow. Change upon change—yet one change cries out to another, like the alternate Seraphim, in praise and in glory of their Maker. The sun sinks to rise again; the day is swallowed up in the gloom of the night, to be born out of it, as fresh as if it had never been quenched. Spring passes into summer, and through summer and autumn into winter, only the more surely, by its own ultimate return, to triumph over that grave, towards which it resolutely hastened from its first hour. We mourn over the blossoms of May, because they are to wither; but we know, withal, that May is one day to have its revenge upon November, by the revolution of that solemn circle which never stops—which teaches us in our height of hope, ever to be sober, and in our depth of desolation, never to despair.

John Henry Newman
Nineteenth century

As long as the earth endures,
        seedtime and harvest, cold and heat,
summer and winter, day and night,
        shall not cease.

Genesis 8:22

WE can, over time, become enthralled in the trance of our work. It is all-important, it must be done right away, it won't get done without me, I cannot stop or it will all fall apart, it is all up to me, terrible things will happen if I do not get this done. I have to keep working because I have things to buy and there are bills to pay for those things and I have to buy faster computers and more expensive telephones to help me get more done so I can keep up and make money to pay the bills for the things I need to buy to help me get these things done . . .

Once we are in this trance, there never seems to be a good enough reason to stop. The wisdom of Sabbath time is that at a prescribed moment, it is time to stop. We cannot wait until we are finished, because we are never finished. We cannot wait until we have everything we need, because the mind is seduced by endlessly multiplying desires. We cannot wait until things slow down, because the world is moving faster and faster, and we cannot be left behind. There are always a million good reasons to keep on going, and never a good enough reason to stop.

Wayne Muller
Twentieth century

OUR calendars are filled with appointments, our days and weeks filled with engagements, and our years filled with plans and projects. There is seldom a period in which we do not know what to do, and we move through life in such a distracted way that we do not even take the time and rest to wonder if any of the things we think, say, or do are *worth* thinking, saying, or doing. We simply go along with the many "musts" and "oughts" that have been handed on to us. . . .

Why do we children of the light so easily become conspirators with the darkness? The answer is quite simple. Our identity, our sense of self, is at stake. Secularity is a way of being dependent on the responses of our milieu. The secular or false self is the self which is fabricated, as Thomas Merton says, by social compulsions. "Compulsive" is indeed the best adjective for the false self. It points to the need for ongoing and increasing affirmation. Who am I? I am the one who is liked, praised, admired, disliked, hated, or despised.

Whether I am a pianist, a businessman or a minister, what matters is how I am perceived by my world.

Henri Nouwen
Twentieth century

HOW many have relinquished
Breath, in grief or rage,
The victor and the vanquished
Named on the bitter page

Alike, or indifferently
Forgot—all that they did
Undone entirely.
The dust they stirred has hid

Their faces and their works,
Has settled, and lies still.
Nobody rests or shirks
Who must turn in time's mill.

They wind the turns of the mill
In house and field and town;
As grist is ground to meal
The grinders are ground down.

Wendell Berry
Twentieth century

IN a contrary and perhaps rather cruel way the twentieth century has relieved us of labor without at the same time relieving us of the conviction that only labor is meaningful.

Walter Kerr
Twentieth century

MY father didn't just preach non-stop work, he modeled it. For the last 15 of his 62 years, he painted houses. We lived in Phoenix then, and he often started work at 5 a.m. to beat the heat. Several of my younger siblings worked with him—before school, after school, weekends—giving up childhood's normal diversions to paint and sand and wash the brushes.

"You have a family of little worker bees, don't you?" a friend's mother once said. I glowered at her, but proudly.

Work was our family virtue, our collective identity. For years, I brought that to my paying jobs—Work 'til midnight? Sign me up!—and into my home life. . . .

Finally, a few years ago, I began to think that maybe a little less effort would yield different but equal rewards. Perhaps the work ethic my father instilled in us was in some ways just a work compulsion. He had no hobbies, no extracurricular pleasures, no means of relaxing except his Camels and Christian Brothers burgundy and TV football games.

In some measure, work and its stresses killed him, along with the co-conspirators of cigarettes and alcohol, all of which finally added up to cancer.

I admired his capacity for work; still do. . . .

But if I could have granted my father one wish—my wish—it would have been that he learn to find pleasure and meaning in something beyond work.

Mary Schmich
Twentieth century

WE eat fast foods and wonder why we are still hungry. We snatch winks and wonder why we are not refreshed. We work without imagination and wonder why we are uninspired. We never stop. We turn constantly and wonder why we are dizzy.

Georgene L. Wilson
Twentieth century

LIFE goes wrong when the control of space, the acquisitions of things of space, becomes our sole concern. . . .

We are all infatuated with the splendor of space, with the grandeur of things of space. Thing is a category that lies heavy on our minds, tyrannizing all our thoughts. Our imagination tends to mold all concepts in its image. In our daily lives we attend primarily to that which the senses are spelling out for us: to what the eyes perceive, to what the fingers touch. Reality to us is thinghood, consisting of substances that occupy space; even God is conceived by most of us as a thing.

The result of our thinginess is our blindness to all reality that fails to identify itself as a thing, as a matter of fact. This is obvious in our understanding of time, which, being thingless and insubstantial, appears to us as if it had no reality.

Indeed, we know what to do with space but do not know what to do about time, except to make it subservient to space. Most of us seem to labor for the sake of things of space. As a result we suffer from a deeply rooted dread of time and stand aghast when compelled to look into its face. Time to us is sarcasm, a slick treacherous monster with a jaw like a furnace incinerating every moment of our lives. Shrinking, therefore, from facing time, we escape for shelter to things of space. The intentions we are unable to carry out we deposit in space; possessions become the symbols of our repressions, jubilees of frustrations. But things of space are not fireproof; they only add fuel to the flames. Is the joy of possession an antidote to the terror of time which grows to be a dread of inevitable death? Things, when magnified, are forgeries of happiness, they are a threat to our very lives; we are more harassed than supported by the Frankensteins of spatial things.

Abraham Joshua
Heschel
Twentieth century

I can't understand it. My sister in the capital, she now has all these things that do the work faster. She just buys clothes in a shop, she has a jeep, a telephone, a gas cooker. All of these things save so much time, and yet when I go to visit her, she doesn't have time to talk to me.

Ladakhi Villager,
Northeast Kashmir
Twentieth century

IT isn't only work that labels and identifies us. *Tu sei quello che fai* (You are what you do). We are known, identified, and labeled by what we consume, purchase or buy. *L'uomo e'quello che compra* (Every man is what he buys, or You are what you buy). In an advertisement-intense, capitalistic economy people are known by *where* they shop, *how* they shop and *what* they buy and own. More than a century ago Henry David Thoreau observed that "Americans know more about how to make a living than how to live." By and large, his critique remains true today. We organize our lives around our economic institutions and measure our value and worth by our success on the job and our choices as consumers. . . .

We love to shop, we want to shop, and, at a very basic level, we need to shop and consume. The desire to consume is not wrong. Critics of the consumer economy are not simply attacking every pleasure that can be associated with products or services that we need. The issue is not consumerism itself, but consumption as an addiction, an obsession, or a metaphysical orientation toward life.

Al Gini
Twentieth century

IF the inhabitants of the world have suffered from the inequitable distribution of food, goods and land, we have also suffered from the lack of a mode of relating to the world that might be born of sanctified time. Almost 2000 years ago, talmudic mystics spoke to the conflict that is lived out in the forum of vast numbers of human souls: When the heavens and earth were called into existence, they wrote, matter was getting out of hand, and the divine voice had to resound, "Enough! So far, and no further!" Today, I believe, the voice continues to resound, and to address the empty centers of distorted life with a goal and a way. Today, Jews, along with many Christians, have again gone in search of meaningful grounding. Some of us want to distill the traditions that can help us recapture the real.

For me, as for my forebears, the Sabbath as event remains a path to healing. It is a way of facing separation and meeting, death and rebirth, and other significant processes of life through the tools of real relating—presence, listening, imagination, response and reparation. For me, as for my forebears, the Sabbath embodies a concern for inner unity and interhuman equity through the tools of personal piety—study, song, and prayer.

Barbara R. Krasner
Twentieth century

A saying: Cain's true punishment? He unlearned the meaning of Shabbat.

Elie Wiesel
Twentieth century

TIME. Jews have an amazing way with time. We create islands of time. Rope it off. Isolate it. Put it on another plane. In doing so, we create within that time a special aura around our everyday existence. Carving out special segments of holy time suits the human psyche perfectly, for ordinary human beings cannot live constantly at the peak of emotion. Thus, Shabbat, holy time, gives us an opportunity to experience that emotional peak, to feel something extraordinary in an otherwise ordinary span of time.

You would not think of time as having texture, yet in a traditional Jewish household it becomes almost palpable. On Shabbat, I can almost feel the difference in the air I breath, in the way the incandescent lamps give off light in my living room, in the way the children's skins glow, or the way the trees sway. Immediately after I light my candles, it is as if I flicked a switch that turned Shabbat on in the world, even though I know very well the world is not turned on to Shabbat. Remarkable as this experience is, even more remarkable is that it happens every seventh day of my life.

Blu Greenberg
Twentieth century

CAN we ever get a good common prayer at Sunday liturgy when we expect to make it all happen between the opening and closing of the church doors? That hour needs an environment, a setting. Our best efforts for good Sunday liturgy will inevitably come up against this: people cannot prepare to DO something between the holy water font and the first reading. Good liturgy is people DOING. Without that, it may be fine ceremony and grand music, but not good liturgy. . . .

Only something that happens outside that hour, that surrounds it, can create the energy and desire to gather around that table and DO our eucharist with all these folks. That something is the Sunday. . . .

All the skills for this work of common prayer cannot be picked up in the big Sunday congregation. They must be brought to the liturgy by persons who are learning what it is to pray in common in the tiny assembly of the household.

Gabe Huck
Twentieth century

ONCE, when I was seeking the advice of Howard Thurman and talking to him at some length about what needed to be done in the world, he interrupted me and said: "Don't ask yourself what the world needs. Ask yourself what makes you come alive, and go do that, because what the world needs is people who have come alive."

Gil Bailie
Twentieth century

Six days you shall labor and do all your work.   Exodus 20:9

THE light was slowly coming up behind the trees. Lili could hear the whispers of the market women, their hisses and swearing as their sandals dug into the sharp-edged rocks on the road.

She turned her back to her husband as she slipped out of her nightgown, quickly putting on her day clothes. . . .

Lili shut the door behind her, making her way out to the yard. The empty gasoline containers rested easily on her head as she walked a few miles to the public water foun-tains. It was harder to keep them steady when the containers were full. The water splashed all over her blouse and rippled down her back.

The sky was blue as it was most mornings, a dark indigo-shaded turquoise that would get lighter when the sun was fully risen.

Guy and the boy were standing in the yard waiting for her when she got back.

"You did not get much sleep, my handsome boy," she said, running her wet fingers over the boy's face.

"He'll be late for school if we do not go right now," Guy said. "I want to drop him off before I start work.". . .

Lili watched them walk down the footpath, her eyes fol-lowing them until they disappeared.

As soon as they were out of sight, she poured the water she had fetched into a large calabash, letting it stand beside the house.

She went back into the room and slipped into a dry blouse. It was never too early to start looking around, to scrape together that night's meal.

Edwidge Danticat
Twentieth–Twenty-first
century

MY mother and father are Neopolitan. Actually, they're from just outside Naples, in the Provincia di Salerno. They came to America, with hundreds of thousands of other Italians, in the late twenties, illiterate, without money or property and with only a few friends. My father worked awhile in New Jersey, cleaning what were euphemistically called trenches: they were in fact sewers. He was like most of the other immigrants: powerless but prideful; anguished by a lack of education but ambitious; frightened by a society he didn't know but forceful about making his way in. And always, cursed with that unrelenting Italian passion, the passion for the family; a driving desire to sacrifice a large part of his own life only to make something better for his children; that ultimate humility that gives up nearly everything to the next generation.

By the time he and my mother had their third child, it was clear to him that he would have to do something more than dig "trenches" to provide what he wanted for his family. He opened a grocery store with the few pennies they had saved. . . .

The store was open twenty-four hours a day, and by the time I was born in 1932, during the Depression, my father was making a living from sandwiches he made in the early morning for the construction crews and quick midnight snacks he prepared for the night shift in the factory across the street. In between, his store was the neighborhood corner grocery. . . .

. . . He taught us all about the dignity of work and man's instinct to survive by his own hand wherever possible. No monk bearing the inscription "to labor is to pray" could have taught us more.

Mario Cuomo
Twentieth century

GOD, bless Thou Thyself my reaping,
Each ridge, and plain, and field,
Each sickle curved, shapely, hard,
Each ear and handful in the sheaf,
  Each ear and handful in the sheaf.

Gaelic prayer

I T is about ulcers as well as accidents, about shouting matches as well as fistfights, about nervous breakdowns as well as kicking the dog around. It is, above all (or beneath all), about daily humiliations. To survive the day is triumph enough for the walking wounded among the great many of us. . . .

It is about a search, too, for daily meaning as well as daily bread, for recognition as well as cash, for astonishment rather than torpor; in short, for a sort of life rather than a Monday through Friday sort of dying. . . .

. . . To earn one's bread by the sweat of one's brow has always been the lot of mankind. At least, ever since Eden's slothful couple was served with an eviction notice. The scriptural precept was never doubted, not out loud. No matter how demeaning the task, no matter how it dulls the senses and breaks the spirit, one *must* work. Or else.

Studs Turkel
Twentieth century

I have just stumbled backward onto the trading floor of the New York Stock Exchange during one of the peaks of the great bull market of the late twentieth century. . . . Two-dollar broker Ed Rode is ready to rock 'n' roll. . . .

Ed and I descended into the Jovian atmosphere together, a three-dimensional space of green flashing "ask" and "bid" prices, CNBC television feeds, and flat panel screens on goosenecks. An emergency cabinet marked "Defibrillator" in urgent letters flies by. Drifts of used order slips make the wooden floor unreliable, so I look up to get my bearings from the heavens, only to find a gently spinning kaleidoscope: a traditional gold leaf ceiling of carved rectangles superimposed with a postmodern burnished aluminum web of pipes from which dangle cables that support the stock trading kiosks. . . .

. . . "Two-dollar brokers" are freelancers, such as Ed. If you want a share of Archer Daniels Midland or something, the word gets through to Ed's people, Richard Rosenblatt and Company, who pass the word to Ed's clerks, who shout or radio to Ed how much you want to buy and at what price. Ed is like your personal shopper at the mall of stocks, and it is his job to take your order over to the third kind of broker on the floor, "the specialist," and bid for you. . . .

It's the next afternoon, a cold one back in the financial district. For eight months a year, Wayne works as a custodian in the New York City public school system. From January through April every year, he runs a small business shining shoes along the wrought-iron fence that surrounds Trinity Church at the top of Wall Street. I wonder if he gets any tips.

He replies that he is always happy to accept a gratuity. . . .

From April to December, the custodian job provides a take-home pay of $800 and change every two weeks. Most important, it is a job that provides medical benefits for the family and a contribution to Social Security.

"Shine 'em up. Shine 'em up."

Wayne's cousin stops by. Donnell is older and works as a runner at one of the houses of finance here. Donnell says he owns a little stock himself. I want to know if you can tell from the collective attitude of the four o'clock throngs whether the market has closed up or down. Donnell has no doubt. It's 3:59 PM.

"Anybody you see rushing for the PATH train, they had a bad day. If you see them taking their time, you see them *strolling,* you see they got just a little smile, not a big one, then you know it's been good.". . .

Both Wayne and Donnell solemnly agree, the Dow has closed down. A chilly wind blows up through the Wall Street canyon, takes a sharp right, and smacks us in the face.

David Brancaccio
Twentieth century

"When it gets warmer, that's when the stock market picks up," Wayne observes.

A desperate man will often do something he shouldn't. After six months without work, Dan took a job with a doghole mine in Rocky Creek down in southern Logan County. . . . The people who ran the mine at Rocky Creek were not known for their safe practices. They had a loose-rock formation above the seam of coal and the men worked in constant danger of roof falls.

Dan put in two weeks as foreman on the day shift. One day he kept the section idle because the roof-bolter was slow in securing a newly opened area. When the superintendent told Dan to move the cutting machine into the new area, Dan refused. He said he wasn't going to move men or machines into the area until the roof was secure. The super-intendent got mad and ordered the roof-bolter out of the section and ordered the cutting machine moved in. He was under orders to move coal that day; no foreman was going to slow him down. The super told Dan he would have another crew erect timber supports while the cutting machine was loosening coal.

"Be my guest," Dan snapped, moving outside the mine. "I don't want to have any part of it."

A few hours later, while working in the office, Dan heard an awful scream. He rushed inside and saw a machine helper lying on the floor, his face bleeding badly from a falling rock. The wound stopped bleeding after a while and the injury was not serious. But Dan knew it could have been worse. . . .

Dan drove straight home and told Margaret he had quit. She started to cry. She said she knew he did the right thing. But she cried and cried.

George Vecsey
Twentieth century

Y OU eatin' lunch early today, Mr. C.?
  Brown baggin' it, I see. Mind if I join you?
Me, I got peanut butter again.
No, life ain't been too good lately.
My father just lost his job at the plant.
He's been with the company nearly thirty years
And suddenly they close the place, just like that.
Where's a fifty-five-year-old man gonna find another job?

It's killing him.
My mother got a job at the local Seven-Eleven.
She says the customers are crazy.
She's on her feet all day.
It's killing her.
I've been trying to find work too,
But no luck. Know of anything?
I think my family's dying by degrees.
I better get used to peanut butter.

Mel Glenn
Twentieth century

T HEY mow the lawn every ten minutes at Microsoft. It
  looks like green Lego pads.

At about 2:30 AM, Todd and I got concerned about
Michael's not eating, so we drove to the 24-hour Safeway
in Redmond. We went shopping for "flat" foods to slip
underneath Michael's door.

The Safeway was completely empty save for us and a few
other Microsoft people just like us—hair-trigger geeks in
pursuit of just the right snack. Because of all the rich nerds
living around here, Redmond and Bellevue are very "on-
demand" neighborhoods. Nerds get what they want when
they want it, and they go psycho if it's not immediately
available. Nerds overfocus. I guess that's the problem. But
it's precisely this ability to narrow-focus that makes them so
good at code writing: one line at a time, one line in a strand
of millions.

When we returned to Building Seven at 3:00 AM, . . .

Michael's office lights were on, but once again, when we knocked he wouldn't answer his door. We heard his keyboard chatter, so we figured he was still alive. . . . We slid Kraft singles, Premium Plus crackers, Pop Tarts, grape leather, and Freezie-Pops in to him.

By this point Todd and I were both really tired. We drove back to the house to crash, each in our separate cars, through the Campus grounds—22 buildings' worth of nerd-cosseting fun—cloistered by 100-foot-tall second growth timber, its streets quiet as the womb: the foundry of our culture's deepest dreams.

Douglas Coupland
Twentieth century

Our life is ruled by time. The millennium celebrations do not let us forget that! But as a Jew, my time is ruled by another calendar. And we have to work at juggling the demands made by both.

Even the small differences are important. Our day begins at sunset. We don't have to wait till the bewitching hour to start a festival! On the eve of a Sabbath or festival we experience what I, as a science fiction fan, call the 'Star Trek' effect. I rush in from synagogue; the family is busy with their own activities. The television is usually still on. Over that noise our son is playing the piano. I bustle like mad about the kitchen finishing off our dinner. After a few hectic and rather tense moments we gather round the table. And my daughter and I light the candles.

It is as if we have been transported to another world. Suddenly, we have time for each other. My husband recites the kiddush, the prayer that sanctifies the day, and blesses the children and pays tribute to my contribution to the family in the words from the book of Proverbs: ['A woman of worth, who can find her? Her price is far above rubies.'] And, as a family, often with guests, we can sit and talk about our week, our plans, sometimes even about what has been learnt about the reading for the Sabbath day. The Sabbath peace has arrived and normal activities, shopping, writing, cooking, spending money, cease until three stars have appeared in the sky on Saturday evening.

Then the process is reversed. Again we use candles and wine, though this time we add the sweet smell of the spices to remind our Sabbath souls that a return visit will be worth it next week! And as we sing farewell to the peace we have enjoyed, so the computers go back on, the phone starts ringing and the mad hectic lifestyle we all seem to endure these days begins again.

But Shabbat does not just begin at sunset on Friday. If we left preparations until then, how could we enjoy the day? The whole week is built around it; from what shall we eat? (Food again!) What visitors shall we invite? To when can we shop? Cook? And organize ourselves so we can be free to enjoy? Not only that. The Torah reading on the Sabbath is so much more meaningful if it has been studied in advance. And even prayer needs daily practice. *Especially* prayer needs daily practice. We cannot expect the Sabbath prayers to have meaning without the daily spiritual workout. . . .

And if the Sabbath relies on preparation, physical and spiritual, to take place on the working days of the week, so the festivals rely on the Sabbaths and each other to make a meaningful and coherent whole.

Jackie Tabick
Twentieth century

ALL praise be yours, God our Creator,
as we wait in joyful hope
for the flowering of justice
and the fullness of peace.
All praise for this day, this Friday.
By our weekly fasting and prayer,
cast out the spirit of war, of fear and mistrust,
and make us grow hungry for human kindness,
thirsty for solidarity with all the people of your dear earth.
May all our prayer, our fasting, and our deeds
be done in the name of Jesus.

Gabe Huck
Twentieth century

So whenever you give alms, do not sound a trumpet before you, as the hypocrites do in the synagogues and in the streets, so that they may be praised by others. Truly I tell you, they have received their reward. But when you give alms, do not let your left hand know what your right hand is doing, so that your alms may be done in secret; and your Father who sees in secret will reward you.

And whenever you pray, do not be like the hypocrites; for they love to stand and pray in the synagogues and at the street corners, so that they may be seen by others. Truly I tell you, they have received their reward. But whenever you pray, go into your room and shut the door and pray to your Father who is in secret; and your Father who sees in secret will reward you.

And whenever you fast, do not look dismal, like the hypocrites, for they disfigure their faces so as to show others that they are fasting. Truly I tell you, they have received their reward. But when you fast, put oil on your head and wash your face, so that your fasting may be seen not by others but by your Father who is in secret; and your Father who sees in secret will reward you.

Matthew 6:2–6, 16–18

Do you know the Hopkins-Bridges correspondence? [ROBERT] Bridges wrote [Gerard Manley] Hopkins at one point and asked him how he could possibly learn to believe, expecting, I suppose, a metaphysical answer. Hopkins only said, "Give alms."

Flannery O'Connor
Twentieth century

Come then; dispose of your wealth in various directions. . . . Do not press heavily on necessity and sell for great prices. Do not wait for a famine before you open your barns. . . . Watch not for a time of want for gold's sake, for public scarcity to promote your private profit. Drive not a huckster's bargain out of the troubles of humankind. Make not God's wrathful visitation an opportunity for abundance.

Saint Basil
Fourth century

THERE is none so poor that he cannot help his fellows. We have a friend down the street who lives in a little apartment for about 12 dollars a month. When she can get the work to do, she does housework, day work, the hardest kind, to earn her bread. She brought in some men's shoes and clothes that she had begged for us from her employers. Another woman in the neighborhood who has four children, a husband with a fractured skull and yet does not have the necessities of life, brought in some children's clothes to be passed on. Another mother, on relief herself, brought in some children's coats.

Dorothy Day
Twentieth century

OYSTERS and lobsters, poor men's fare till the late nineteenth century, have now become exceedingly *chic*. But fish has traditionally been so low on the scale that it was commonly permitted in such religious strategies as Lenten abstinence or the Catholic institution of "fish on Fridays." Lowering one's sights from meat to fish was an exercise in humility, and designed to raise consciousness by elected self-restraint, and by forcing oneself to remember.

Margaret Visser
Twentieth century

ONE reason for the custom of not eating meat on Fridays is as an act of respect for creation. After all, on this day all the "cattle and creeping things, and wild animals of all kinds" were created—and we, too, were created. Created on the same day, are we to devour one another? (Fish, of course, were not created on the sixth day. Devouring them on Fridays even became for Christians a way to anticipate the heavenly banquet when that largest of sea creatures, Leviathan [see Isaiah 27:1 and Psalm 74:14], the very embodiment of evil, will be slain and served up to the saved.)

Surely another reason for the Friday fast is a way to recollect the dreadful consequences of irresponsible eating in Eden. Fasting on Fridays is a sign of great sorrow for sin, the sin for which we were kicked out of Eden, the sin that took the bridegroom from us, the sin of infidelity and broken promises, whenever we turn our backs on our own baptism. What are our baptismal vows if not wedding vows? We pledge to love each other as we love Christ, as bride and groom "till death do us part."

Fasting on Friday is also a sign of great joy for grace. For we are invited to return to paradise and stand before the tree of life, the cross of Christ. In the gracious life of Easter we believe that even death will not dissolve this marriage between Christ and ourselves. It was on a Friday that the Spirit of life was breathed into dead clay (Genesis 2:7). And it was on a Friday that the Spirit of Jesus was given to us from the cross (John 19:30). . . .

. . . Some people think that the church did away with Friday fasting, but that's simply not so. Modern church law (canons 1249–1253) challenges us to keep Fridays with fasting and abstinence from meat as well as special prayer, self-denial and works of mercy. The law permits the national conferences of bishops to be more specific about the nature of Friday observance. The bishops of the United States have done just that, asking us to pray, fast and do works of charity on Fridays for the sake of peace in our homes and communities, in our country and our world.

In the long tradition of the church, we are called to make Friday a day we dedicate to restoring the earth to Eden: in peace, in simplicity, in harmony. We are called to stop wasting both human and natural resources. We are called to wholesomeness, to turn away from consumerism, to stop whatever pollutes both ourselves and our planet. That perhaps is one of the most powerful reasons to fast.

Such fasting is in every sense a turning away from sin and a living of the gospel. The Friday fast is but the necessary first course to both the sabbath rest and the Sunday feast.

Peter Mazar
Twentieth century

WE come to you in penitence, confessing our sins: the vows we have forgotten, the opportunities we have let slip, the excuses whereby we have sought to deceive ourselves and you. Forgive us that we talk so much and are silent so seldom; that we are in such constant motion and are so rarely still; that we depend so implicitly on the effectiveness of our organizations and so little on the power of your Spirit. Teach us to wait upon you, that we may renew our strength, mount up with wings as eagles, run and not be weary, walk and not faint.

William Sloane Coffin Jr.
Twentieth century

ALL night had shout of men and cry
   Of woeful women filled his way;
Until that noon of sombre sky
   On Friday, clamour and display
Smote him; no solitude had he,
No silence, since Gethsemane.

Public was Death; but Power, but Might,
   But Life again, but Victory,
Were hushed within the dead of night,
   The shuttered dark, the secrecy.
And all alone, alone, alone,
He rose again behind the stone.

Alice Meynell
Nineteenth century

AS it is, we do not yet see everything in subjection to them, but we do see Jesus, who for a little while was made lower than the angels, now crowned with glory and honor because of the suffering of death, so that by the grace of God he might taste death for everyone.

Hebrews 2:8c–9

CHRIST our Savior canceled the debt
that pledged us to the decrees of the Law
by nailing it (with Himself) to the Cross,
and He put down the dominion of death.
We worship His Resurrection on the third day.

Byzantine liturgy

MY love gave me a king's robe,
Mock purple and red;
My love gave me a white coat,
A fool's coat, he said;
My love gave me a weft crown
Of thorns for my head.
Because he is my true love
He wore them instead.

M. Madaleva, csc
Twentieth century

WHEN the wood of the Cross, itself the innocent victim
and unchoosing collaborator in man's inhumanity to
man, became the means of expressing a hitherto undreamed
of relationship between God and his people, the wood itself
was redeemed.

Mark Searle
Twentieth century

THOUSANDS of geese dropped down, squadrons
of perfect V's gliding over willows
without leaves. Back from Canada, they fanned out

over the grass, eating whatever geese eat
after thousands of miles on the flyway.
From the office, we saw them flocked in the park

like cobblestones. Families tossed scraps of bread,
surrounded. Toddlers turned their backs,
hands to their heads, gasping, begging for help.

After work, we crossed the hospital parking lot
and watched dogs parting the flocks,
their masters calling. Hundreds of geese

flapped away, but not far, banking back
to the lake, a mile of feathers and bowed necks
dipping and feeding, the whole world honking.

Across the road at the rest home, old people
in wheelchairs lined the sidewalks, wheels locked
and alone, or pushed by their children or aides.

Most pointed and waved. Some merely slumped,
heads bowed and limp, as if asleep,
now that they'd seen these wild, exotic wings.

Walt McDonald
Twentieth century

ONE evening rush hour during my eighth month I was waiting for a train at Columbus Circle. The loudspeaker was crackling unintelligibly and ominously and there were as many people on the platform as currently live in Santa Barbara, Calif. Suddenly I had the dreadful feeling that I was being surrounded. "To get mugged at a time like this," I thought ruefully. "And this being New York, they'll probably try to take the baby, too." But as I looked around I saw that the people surrounding me were four women, some armed with shoulder bags. "You need protection," one said, and being New Yorkers, they ignored the fact that they did not know one another and joined forces to form a kind of phalanx around me, not unlike those that offensive linemen build around a quarterback.

When the train arrived and the doors opened, they moved forward, with purpose, and I was swept inside, not the least bit bruised. "Looks like a boy," said one with a grin, and as the train began to move, we all grabbed the silver overhead handles and turned away from one another.

Anna Quindlen
Twentieth century

S HE said, If tomorrow my world were torn in two,
Blacked out, dissolved, I think I would remember
(As if transfixed in unsurrendering amber)
This hour best of all the hours I knew:
When cars came backing into the shabby station,
Children scuffing the seats, and the women driving
With ribbons around their hair, and the trains arriving,
And the men getting off with tired but practiced motion.

Yes, I would remember my life like this, she said:
Autumn, the platform red with Virginia creeper,
And a man coming toward me, smiling, the evening paper
Under his arm, and his hat pushed back on his head;
And wood smoke lying like haze on the quiet town,
And dinner waiting, and the sun not yet gone down.

Phyllis McGinley
Twentieth century

I leant upon a coppice gate
    When Frost was spectre-gray,
And Winter's dregs made desolate
    The weakening eye of day.
The tangled bine-stems scored the sky
    Like strings of broken lyres,
And all mankind that haunted nigh
    Had sought their household fires.

The land's sharp features seemed to be
    The Century's corpse outleant,
His crypt the cloudy canopy,
    The wind his death-lament.
The ancient pulse of germ and birth
    Was shrunken hard and dry,
And every spirit upon earth
    Seemed fervourless as I.

At once a voice arose among
    The bleak twigs overhead

In a full-hearted evensong
   Of joy illimited;
An aged thrush, frail, gaunt, and small,
   In a blast-beruffled plume,
Had chosen thus to fling his soul
   Upon the growing gloom.

So little cause for carollings
   Of such ecstatic sound
Was written on terrestrial things
   Afar or nigh around,
That I could think there trembled through
   His happy good-night air
Some blessed Hope, whereof he knew
   And I was unaware.

Thomas Hardy
Nineteenth century

WHEN icicles hang by the wall,
      And Dick the shepherd blows his nail,
And Tom bears logs into the hall,
   And milk comes frozen home in pail,
When blood is nipp'd, and ways be foul,
Then nightly sings the staring owl,
      Tu-whit;
Tu-who, a merry note,
While greasy Joan doth keel the pot.

When all aloud the wind doth blow,
   And coughing drowns the parson's saw,
And birds sit brooding in the snow,
   And Marian's nose looks red and raw,
When roasted crabs hiss in the bowl,
Then nightly sings the staring owl,
      Tu-whit;
Tu-who, a merry note,
While greasy Joan doth keel the pot.

William Shakespeare
Sixteenth century

ON the sixth ev'ning you gave back
the human spirit you once gave,
that we might all receive again
the life that saves us from the grave.

Thus in the garden of the cross
the tree of death its fruit bestows,
and now the Spirit may be giv'n
that only comes when he arose.

O Lord of life and Lord of death,
hell's Visitor, all souls release;
to you be ev'ry glory giv'n
through all the ages without cease.

Aelred Squire, OSB CAM
Twentieth century

WITH shadows death foreshadowing,
now full upon this fading day,
O Abba, God, our lives enfold
and keep us safe in sleep, we pray.

Those phantom fears which flood the heart
cast out—and dwell more richly there.
Weave dreams, those healing heralds of
your kingdom to which we are heir.

Your glory be a flame this night,
a light to our mortality.
In your embrace we rest secure,
till at the last, your face we see.

Aelred Seton-Shanley
Twentieth century

Blu Greenberg
Twentieth century

A friend has this bumper sticker affixed to the front of her refrigerator: HANG IN THERE, SHABBOS IS COMING. There definitely are weeks in my life when I feel that I will barely make it, but the prize of Shabbat carries me through.

Code of Jewish Law

EVEN the poorest man in Israel should endeavor with all his might to luxuriate in the Sabbath. He should economize the whole week to save enough money for the Sabbath meals. If necessary, one should even borrow money on a pledge in order to provide for the Sabbath. Of such a person, our Rabbis, of blessed memory, say (Betzah 15a): "Said the Holy One, blessed be He, to His people Israel: 'My children, borrow for My sake and I will repay you.'"

Leo Rosten
Twentieth century

AND so, for Sabbath, down the generations, in every land, Jews have scrubbed every nook of their dwelling, bathed themselves with the utmost care, donned fresh garments, laid out (however poor) their best linens, glasses, utensils. *Shabbes* brought—each week, throughout a lifetime—a sense of personal splendor, cleanliness, devotion, exaltation.

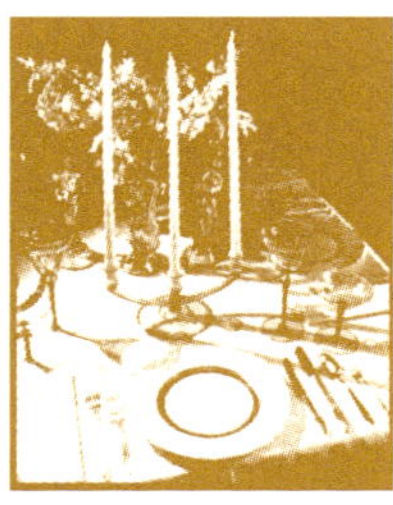

AT the Konigsberg house, twenty-five minutes before sundown, Sheina, dressed in an elegant tan silk blouse and tweed skirt, was preparing to light the Sabbath candles. . . .

According to custom, Sabbath candles are lit twenty minutes before sundown. The meal had been cooked, the table elaborately set, the heavy, ornately wrought silver candelabrum polished, and the family and some guests were milling around the living room. . . .

The activities proscribed for the Sabbath either by the Bible or by post-Biblical decree seem mind-boggling to outsiders. They include cooking; baking; washing laundry; chopping;

knitting; crocheting; sewing; embroidering; pasting; drawing; painting; writing; typing; fishing; hunting; cutting hair (or cutting anything else, with the exception of food); building or repairing anything; gardening; carrying or pushing anything farther than six feet in public; riding in cars, planes, trains, or buses; boating; buying or selling; horseback riding; playing a musical instrument; switching on any electrical apparatus, such as a TV set, phonograph or radio; handling any objects whose use is forbidden on the Sabbath, such as money, tools, or pencils; exercising or playing any sport; or traveling, even by foot, more than a short distance from the place where one is ensconced on the Sabbath. I asked Sheina how she felt about having her activities so restricted each week. Surveying the dinner table approvingly, as the men filed out the door to go to their evening service, she replied that she didn't think of it that way.

"I feel that I'm getting a break," she said, as she placed a heavy water pitcher on the table. "Once you get some of the more complicated things out of the way, like the food cooking in advance and setting a large urn of hot water on a metal cover over a low burner so that everybody can have coffee and tea to drink on Saturday, and covering some of the light switches so that no one will accidentally turn the important lights off, it feels more like a holiday. What if you were flown to a quiet tropical island every week? Wouldn't you be pleased if you were permitted, even obliged, to just put aside your everyday burdens and everyday chores? I don't really know what other people's lives are like, but I doubt that most families get the chance we do to just sit around and talk to one another every weekend. On weekends most Americans seem to play as hard as they work."

Lis Harris
Twentieth century

COME, my Shabbas Queen,
embodiment of Worlds-to-Be:
Your gracious kindness is our breath of life,
and though we once, twice, all-too-often
fail to say, "How beautiful your cape!
How lovely your hair, your Shechina-eyes!"

we will not always be so lax,
apathetic to your grace, your presence.
Touch us again this week
with your most unique love's tenderness,
and we shall sing to you our songs,
dance our dances in your honor,
and sigh for you our sighs
of longing, peace and hope.

Danny Siegel
Twentieth century

WHEN the world was created, Shabbat said to the Holy One, "Ruler of the Universe, every living thing created has its mate, and each day has its companion, except me, the seventh day. I am alone!" God answered, " The people of Israel will be your mate."

When the Israelites arrived at Mount Sinai, the Holy One said to them, "Remember what I said to Shabbat—that the people of Israel would be her mate?" It is with reference to this that My fourth commandment for you reads: "*Remember* the Sabbath day, to keep it holy."

Genesis Rabbah 11:8

THE idea of the Sabbath as a queen or a bride is not a personification of the Sabbath but an exemplification of a divine attribute, an illustration of God's need for human love; it does not represent a substance but the presence of God, His relationship to man.

Such a metaphorical exemplification does not state a fact; it expresses a value, putting into words the preciousness of the Sabbath as Sabbath. Observance of the seventh day is more than a technique of fulfilling a commandment. The Sabbath is the presence of God in the world, open to the soul of man. It is possible for the soul to respond in affection, to enter into fellowship with the consecrated day.

The seventh day was full of both loneliness and majesty— an object of awe, attention and love. Friday eve, when the

Sabbath is about to engross the world, the mind, the entire soul, and the tongue is tied with trembling and joy—what is there that one could say? To those who are not vulgarized, who guard their words from being tainted, queen, bride, signify majesty tempered with mercy and delicate innocence that is waiting for affection.

Abraham Joshua Heschel
Twentieth century

TRADITIONAL Judaism, with its heavy emphasis on role definition, assigned nerot, candlelighting, to women—although not all candles, it must be added. The Havadalah candle, which concludes the Sabbath, and Chanukah candles, the more "public" candles, go to men.

A minimum of two candles are lit, symbolic of the two forms of the commandment—"remember" and "observe" the Sabbath day. Many women light one candle for each member of the family. My mother's candelabrum has five branches. As a child, I used to wonder whether she bought it before or after she had three children.

A woman covers her hair for candlelighting. (Some Orthodox women cover their heads all the time, some only on Shabbat, some only for candlelighting and synagogue attendance.) She then lights the candles but does not blow out the match, laying it down in a safe spot to burn itself out, because the act of candlelighting has ushered Shabbat into her household, and extinguishing the match is no longer permitted.

The ceremony is very simple. A woman encircles the light three times with her hands and repeats with each encircling:

> *Baruch hu u'varuch shemo.*
> Blessed be He and blessed be His name.

She then covers her eyes with both hands and recites the blessing:

Baruch ata Adonai Elohainu melech ha'olam asher kidshanu b'mitzovtav v'tzivanu l'hadlik ner shel Shabbat.

Blessed are You, Lord our God, Ruler of the universe, Who has sanctified us with His commandments and commanded us to kindle the light of the Sabbath.

Blu Greenberg
Twentieth century

Marge Piercy
Twentieth century

THE sweet beeswax candles flicker
and sigh, standing between the phlox
and the roast chicken. The wine shines
its red lantern of joy.

SHE quickly washes her face and hands, puts on a clean lace collar that she always wears on this night, and approaches the candlesticks like a quite new mother. With a match in her hand she lights one candle after another. All the seven candles begin to quiver. The flames blaze into mother's face. As though an enchantment were falling upon her, she lowers her eyes. Slowly, three times in succession, she encircles the candles with both her arms; she seems to be taking them into her heart. And with the candles her weekday worries melt away.

She blesses the candles. She whispers quiet benedictions through her fingers and they add heat to the flames. Mother's hands over the candles shine like the tablets of the decalogue over the holy ark.

I push closer to her. I want to get behind her blessing hands myself. I seek her face. I want to look into her eyes. They are concealed behind her spread-out fingers.

I light my little candle by mother's candle. Like her, I raise my hands and through them, as through a gate, I murmur into my little candle flame the words of benediction that I catch from my mother.

My candle, just lighted, is already dripping. My hands circle it to stop its tears.

I hear mother in her benedictions mention now one name, now another. She names father, the children, her own father and mother. Now my name too has fallen into the flame of the candles. My throat becomes hot.

"May the Highest One give them his blessing!" concludes my mother, dropping her hands at last.

"Amen," I say in a choking voice, behind my fingers.

"Good shabbes!" mother calls out loudly. Her face, all opened, looks purified. I think that it has absorbed the illumination of the Sabbath candles.

Bella Chagall
Twentieth century

I T is good to give thanks to the LORD,
   to sing praises to your name, O Most High;
to declare your steadfast love in the morning,
   and your faithfulness by night,
to the music of the lute and the harp,
   to the melody of the lyre.
For you, O LORD, have made me glad by your work;
   at the works of your hands I sing for joy.

How great are your works, O LORD!
   Your thoughts are very deep!
The dullard cannot know,
   the stupid cannot understand this:
though the wicked sprout like grass
   and all evildoers flourish,
they are doomed to destruction forever,
   but you, O LORD, are on high forever,
For your enemies, O LORD,
   for your enemies shall perish;
   all evildoers shall be scattered.

But you have exalted my horn like that of the wild ox;
   you have poured over me fresh oil.
My eyes have seen the downfall of my enemies;
   my ears have heard the doom of my evil assailants.

The righteous flourish like the palm tree,
   and grow like a cedar in Lebanon.
They are planted in the house of the LORD;
   they flourish in the courts of our God.
In old age they still produce fruit;
   they are always green and full of sap,
showing that the LORD is upright;
   he is my rock, and there is no unrighteousness in him.

Psalm 92

PSALM 92 is a psalm of thanksgiving. It sings the praises of God, who in the fullness of time will destroy the wicked and cause the righteous to blossom forth. It also raises the ancient problem about the prosperity of the wicked and the misfortune of the righteous and answers by saying, appearances to the contrary notwithstanding, the wicked are doomed to destruction, the righteous are destined to endure. The wise understand this; fools do not.

Apart from its title, "Mizmor Shir l'Yom Ha-Shabbat," ("A Psalm, a Song for the Sabbath Day"), there is no other mention of the Sabbath in this psalm. It may have been designated for the Sabbath simply because this was the psalm that the Levites sang in the Temple on the Sabbath day. But inasmuch as its theme of reward and punishment involves the belief in a world-to-come, the title could be a veiled reference to Olam Haba ("world-to-come"), which is described in the Mishnah as a *yom she'kulo Shabbat* ("a day which is all-Sabbath").

Whatever the case, the saying of this psalm marks the formal start of the Sabbath. We stand when saying it, out of deference to the incoming Sabbath, much as we might rise to greet a distinguished visitor upon his entrance.

Hayim Halevy Donin
Twentieth century

WE were everyday Jews in a populated place too tiny even to be a speck on the map. None of us ate more than one decent meal a week, and if the week seemed too long to cope with, too dreary and senseless, we would perk ourselves up a bit thinking of the Sabbath to come—the lighting of the candles at Friday sunset, the beautiful ways the wives had of putting their well-worked palms to their temples, covering their faces for a moment as they uttered the peaceful ritual of the candle-lighting—the dignity of our Sabbath tables, the unity of our clean dear joy, the white cloths, the peace of the shared ecstasy of the Sabbath—the thankful pride in our wives' eyes as we smacked our lips over our savory soup, our slab of meat; and the pudgy curves of the Sabbath loaf baked in twists and jeweled with poppy seeds. Often the loaf did for the week and the soup became thinner and thinner and the nightly potatoes less and less filling, but this only meant that the Sabbath again was nearing.

Peter Martin
Twentieth century

COME, O holy Sabbath evening,
Crown our toil with well earned rest;
Bring us hallowed hours of gladness,
Day of days beloved and blest.

Weave your mystic spell around us
With the glow of Sabbath light:
As we read the ancient wisdom,
Learn its laws of truth and right.

Come, O holy Sabbath spirit,
Radiant shine from every eye;
Lending us your benediction,
Filling every heart with joy.

Gates of Prayer

IN the most populous neighborhood of the world, rent by the shouts of peddlers, the screams of children, and the myriad noises of the city, there was every Friday evening a wondrous stillness, and eloquent silence. So quiet was it that two blocks from the synagogue you could hear the muffled chant of the cantor and the murmured prayers of the congregation. Once the service was over, you came home to find your mother dressed in her wedding dress with a white silk scarf around her head. And your father told you all the sufferings throughout the centuries were dedicated for this moment, the celebration of the Sabbath.

Hutchins Hapgood
Twentieth century

THEY say the pious Sephardic woman, knowing
The Law commands a husband to make love
To his wife on Friday nights, will cook a meal
Contrived to warm his appetite. I almost see
The newly-scrubbed and spotless Sabbath house,
The clean white tablecloths, the braided bread,
Brass candelabra burnished to gold,
The serene flame of twice-blessed candles,
As he enters after prayers, having worshipped
As he should, wearing best shirt, best suit,
The long, quiet Sabbath Saturday
Stretching ahead, and sits at the table
Of his dark-eyed, dark-haired wife
Who quietly says: Eat, eat.

Edwin Zimmerman
Twentieth century

SABBATH brings the joy of the future life into the shtetl. This is the climax of the week, "a different world, no worry, no work.". . . Any delicacy that one finds during the week should be bought and kept, if possible, "for Sabbath."

. . . None must work, none must mourn, none must worry, none must hunger on that day. Any Jew who lacks a Sabbath meal should be helped by those who have more than he. But of course one hopes not to need help, for no matter how poor a man may be he counts on the Lord to provide for the Sabbath meal. Some stroke of luck, some sudden opportunity to earn the price of a fish. . . . Many stories and legends describe miracles by which God at the last moment provided Sabbath fare for a devout Jew who lacked means to "make Sabbath."

. . . Whoever he is, any stranger in need will come to the synagogue on Friday evening and at the end of the service he will expect to be invited to some home. . . . There is a legend that every Sabbath God sends the prophet Elijah, dressed as a needy stranger, to visit the Jews and observe the way they are fulfilling His Commandments. Accordingly the stranger one brings home may be the prophet. No legend is required, however, to stimulate Sabbath hospitality. Prophet or beggar, to feed the hungry is a "good deed.". . . Therefore, it is a privilege to share the Sabbath feast, even if by ill luck it is a meager one.

Mark Zborowski and
Elizabeth Herzog
Twentieth century

JUDAISM is a *religion of time* aiming at *the sanctification of time.* Unlike the space-minded man to whom time is unvaried, iterative, homogeneous, to whom all hours are alike, qualitiless, empty shells, the Bible senses the diversified character of time. There are no two hours alike. Every hour is unique and the only one given at the moment, exclusive and endlessly precious.

Judaism teaches us to be attached to *holiness in time,* to be attached to sacred events, to learn how to consecrate sanctuaries that emerge from the magnificent stream of a year. The Sabbaths are our great cathedrals.

Abraham Joshua
Heschel
Twentieth century

I leave it to cultural historians to appraise the magnitude of the consequence of an entire people, young and old, spending one day a week, year after year, generation after generation, century after century, in a seminar on religion, morals, ethics, responsibility.

Leo Rosten
Twentieth century

MY friend Jacob told me this story. "When Sheila and I were married, her grandparents gave us a brand-new washer and dryer. It was a very generous gift, and we were very grateful to receive such a blessing for our new home. But when they presented them to us, her grandfather explained that this was a Jewish washer and dryer. 'What makes them Jewish?' I asked, naively. Sheila's grandfather replied with a twinkle, 'They won't work on Shabbat.' "

Wayne Muller
Twentieth century

I N the home, the chief Sabbath ritual has always been the meal. Even the number of Sabbath meals marked off the day as special: in a culture where most people ate two meals a day, custom and eventually religious law required that on the Sabbath one eat three (Mishnah *Shabbbat* 16:2; Babylonian Talmud *Shabbat* 118–119). These meals provided a fixed structure for the Sabbath, and synagogue services, like everything else, had to accommodate themselves to the schedule they created. As early as the time of Josephus it was considered a firm religious custom to begin one's midday meal on the Sabbath no later than noon (Josephus *Life* 54 § 279). These meals had to be fancier and more leisurely than workday meals, and at least since the Middle Ages it has been the custom to prolong them by the singing of table songs devoted to various themes of the Sabbath celebration.

Robert Goldenberg
Twentieth century

A PPROACHING the cottage, we heard the sound of voices singing. We went up the path to the back door of the cottage. The singing was coming from the narrow driveway.

My mother stopped at the door and listened. Then she opened the door and we went inside.

I came out onto the screened-in porch and listened to the wind and the surf. I looked at the porch of the house across the driveway and saw four people seated around a table: David Dinn, his aunt and uncle, and a man I did not recognize at first. He wore a dark suit, a white shirt and dark tie, was clean-shaven, and had thick dark hair and chiseled features. David Dinn's uncle too had on a dark suit and tie. His aunt wore a white dress with a high lace collar and long sleeves; a kerchief covered her hair. They sat around the table singing a slow and mournful-sounding tune. David Dinn, wearing a short-sleeved white shirt open at the throat, sat with his eyes closed, swaying slightly back and forth in his chair. He had a high, thin voice. I could hear him clearly above the deeper voices of the men and the soft, subdued voice of his aunt.

My parents and Jakob Daw came out onto the porch. I asked my mother what the people on the other porch were singing.

"Zemiros," she said. "They sing special songs with their Shabbos meals."

Apious Jew loses his way in a forest late one Friday afternoon. The sun sets and the pious man begins to weep in sorrow, because he will be unable to observe the Sabbath. Suddenly he sees a palace standing amidst the trees. An old man appears and motions wordlessly to the lost Jew to follow him. The old man leads him to a fragrant pool, in which the Jew bathes, and then gives him luxurious raiment to wear in honor of the Sabbath. When the guest tries to ask a question, the old man signals him to be still. Then he leads the wanderer into a chamber that glitters with silver and gold, with pearls and precious stones. From there the guide takes him into a second chamber, where candelabra and chandeliers gleam with the radiance of the seven great lights of the Six Days of Creation. And so the guest wanders, enchanted and bedazzled, from room to room, each more beautifully and splendidly adorned than the one before— until, in the seventh and last chamber, he is approached by seven ancient men who with their white beards resemble a forest of snow-covered oak trees. They welcome him and tell him that with his arrival they now have a minyan [the ten men necessary for a Jewish service to be held]. This bewilders the poor Jew: Here are these seven elders, he is the eighth, and the old man accompanying him makes nine, but nowhere does he see the required tenth man. Yet he vividly senses the tenth everywhere about him, like the radiance of the Divine Presence. And he is seized by overwhelming feelings of fear, of awe and reverence, though of the ordinary kind of fear that makes the limbs tremble, there is in his heart not a trace. Now an elder wearing a royal crown takes his place at the cantor's pulpit and welcomes the Sabbath, chanting with such sweetness that one might think him to be the Psalmist himself. After prayers, the Jew is told to wash his hands, and he is then served meat that tastes like the Wild Ox which the righteous will eat in Paradise, and wine with the taste of the wine reserved for the coming of the Messiah. And thus does he spend the entire Sabbath in the elders' company, in prayer, in singing Sabbath hymns, in study of the Torah. And if he essays even a single word about profane matters, they silence him with a gesture. At the conclusion of the Sabbath, he is given spices to smell which have the fragrance of the Tree of Life. Finally, the old man who has been his guide leads him back out into the forest, and whispers in his ear that he has just been in Paradise. And the elders are Abraham, Isaac, and Jacob, Moses and Aaron, and David and Solomon, and he, the caretaker of the palace, is Eliezer, servant to the Patriarch Abraham. And the tenth for the minyan was the Holy One Himself, Blessed be He.

Chaim Grade
Twentieth century

A rite of passage closes the Sabbath and marks the fact of a new beginning. Recited over a cup of wine and fragrant spices that, according to Maimonides, were meant to sustain the soul through the ordeal of loss and separation, the ritual takes place at the end of a day of self-restriction, reflection and relation. Without denying the pathology of existence, the *havdalah* (separation) ceremony surfaces the health-giving elements and dynamics of life that are enduring if invisible. A plaited candle of many wicks holds high the "lights of fire" (Psalm 19:9) that can illumine our individual paths. Hymns that take the Sabbath on its way acknowledge the intensity of the age-old struggle to live with dignity. They also point to the human resources that, in tandem with the ways and will of God, can transform depletion into motivation, and despair into the awesome fact of redemption from the chaos of existence—here and now.

Barbara R. Krasner
Twentieth century

T HE third meal of the Sabbath, usually held just as it is about to end, eventually developed a special character of its own. This, after all, was an emotionally difficult time; even the world seems mournful at the twilight hour when the so-called third meal takes place, and the Jew's brief escape from an often oppressive economic, social, and political reality was about to end. The holy day was about to give way once again to ordinary reality, but this unhappy consideration was offset by another. By tradition, the Messiah will not arrive on a Sabbath or a Sabbath Eve (Babylonian Talmud *'Eruvin* 43b); on those days, after all, the Jews will be too busy or too restricted to be able to receive him as he ought to be received. The end of the Sabbath, therefore, even though by itself it was a sad time, came to bring with it a kind of consolation: now it was once again possible to hope that the Messiah might be on the way. Under the influence of kabbalistic messianism, the "third meal" came to be a time of serene, meditative song, a time for quiet communal waiting for redemption. The *Havdalah* ("division") ceremony that formally ends the Sabbath came to be associated with the prophet Elijah, who since pre-Christian times has been considered the Messiah's herald. Perhaps in connection with these themes, we already find in the Talmud a prediction that the Messiah would in fact not arrive until all Israel had fully and properly observed two Sabbaths in a row (Babylonian Talmud *Shabbat* 118b). Perhaps as well this is why one early rabbi is reported to have said that observance of the Sabbath is like a foretaste of the pleasures of the world to come (Babylonian Talmud *Berakhot* 57b).

Robert Goldenberg
Twentieth century

W E give thanks for the Sabbath day that now is ending. We are grateful for its many blessings: for peace and joy, rest for the body, and refreshment for the soul. May something of its meaning and message remain with us as we enter the new week, lifting all that we do to a higher plane of holiness, and inspiring us to work with new heart for the coming of the day when Elijah's spirit will herald our redemption from all sadness and every bondage.

Gates of the House

SHABBAT is now over. Much as I love the Shabbat and could not live without it, I am happy to see it go. I feel rested, relaxed, and raring to go. Perhaps I shall keep a bit of the Shabbat serenity with me during the week. But I doubt it. If not, I shall rely on the coming Shabbat to restore an added measure of dignity and peace to my life. . . .

Shabbat in a traditional Jewish household is distinctive from Shabbat in any other setting. . . . It comes fifty-two times more often than any other special day in a Jew's life. As such, it occupies, preoccupies, and marks our lives in ways more pervasive and more encompassing than one would ever imagine. Although we are often not conscious of it ourselves, our very lives revolve around Shabbat, even as we throw ourselves with full energy into the weekday world.

Blu Greenberg
Twentieth century

WE praise You, Eternal God, Sovereign of the universe: You make distinctions, teaching us to distinguish the commonplace from the holy; You create light and darkness, Israel and the nations, the seventh day of rest and the six days of labor.

We praise You, O God: You call us to distinguish the commonplace from the holy. . . .

A good week, a week of peace.

Gates of Prayer   May gladness reign and joy increase.

ONCE again the music is measured by silence. Christ is in the tomb as He was in His mother's womb, and just as that first silence was part of the rhythm that moved forward to the visible coming of Life into the world, this silence in the tomb carries the music forward in three great beats to the hour when Life shall again come out of darkness and sweeten and sanctify the world.

Now, as the music becomes audible again, it returns to its simplest form once more. It is lyrical again; at first only a man's breath stirring the flowers in a garden; and then a single word, the name of a friend spoken with indescribable love.

Caryll Houselander
Twentieth century

IF the Church honors the day of the martyrdom of her children, could she forget the sorrows of Mary on the day after the passion? At the foot of the cross, feeling in her mother's heart the steel-clad points of the nails and lance, the bitterness of the blasphemies, and of the gall offered to drink, she was more than martyr: this is the expression of the holy doctors. The solitude of the following day, the absence of her Jesus, the memory always before her eyes of His passion, His death and burial, pierced her torn heart with a new sword.

Abbé Durand
(paraphrasing
Alexander of Hales)
Nineteenth century

As depicted in Scripture, [Mary] walked by faith, not by sight, asking questions, pondering things in her heart and plunging into the dark night of faith when grief stabbed her to the heart. In those days, the expectation of a messianic king was part of a larger hope for liberation of those suffering from oppressive rule. Luke's infancy narrative gives a particular twist to our memory of Mary's faith by placing her in a key position of partnership with God to bring about this historic promise. The Annunciation scene is nothing less than a prophetic vocation story on the model of the call to Moses at the burning bush. After questioning, she gives her free assent, launching her life on an adventure whose outcome is unknown.

Elizabeth A. Johnson
Twentieth century

THEREFORE the Lord himself will give you this sign: The virgin shall be with child, and bear a son, and shall name him Immanuel.

Isaiah 7:14

WITH the same joyful appearance our Lord looked down on his right, and brought to mind where our Lady stood at the time of his Passion, and he said: Do you wish to see her? And I answered and said: Yes, good Lord, great thanks, if it be your will. . . . And Jesus . . . showed me a spiritual vision of her. Just as before I had seen her small and simple, now he showed her high and noble and glorious and more pleasing to him than all creatures. And so he wishes it to be known that all who take delight in him should take delight in her, and in the delight that he has in her and she in him.

Julian of Norwich
Fourteenth century

I am a rose of Sharon,
　a lily of the valleys.

Song of Solomon 2:1

WITH Mary, [the faithful] learn to stand at the foot of the cross, offering to the Father the sacrifice of Christ and joining to it the offering of their own lives. With Mary, they experience the joy of the resurrection, making their own the words of the Magnificat, which extol the inexhaustible gift of divine mercy in the inexorable flow of time: "His mercy is from age to age upon those who fear him" (Luke 1:50).

Pope John Paul II
Twentieth century

AT the message of the angel, the Virgin Mary received the Word of God in her heart and in her body, and gave Life to the world. Hence she is acknowledged and honored as being truly the Mother of God and Mother of the Redeemer. . . .

Therefore she is also hailed as a pre-eminent and altogether singular member of the Church, and as the Church's model and excellent exemplar in faith and charity.

Dogmatic Constitution on the Church

GOD of mercies,
your only Son, while hanging on the cross,
appointed Mary, his mother,
to be our mother also.

Like her,
and under her loving care,
may your Church grow day by day,
rejoice in the holiness of its children,
and so attract to itself all the peoples of the earth.

We ask this through our Lord Jesus Christ, your Son,
who lives and reigns with you and the Holy Spirit,
one God, for ever and ever.

Roman Missal

Paul Gapp
Twentieth century

I F it's cleanup time, it must be Saturday morning in [Swedish] Andersonville on the North Side of Chicago. At the sound of Sonja Sterlov's bell, merchants are supposed to sweep their sidewalks in observance of a tidy Old World custom.

W EEKENDS in our household were not the rhapsody of leisure enjoyed by so many of our friends. "Today's a workday!" my father would proclaim. . . . So, while our friends were playing tennis or lounging at the pool or lurking at the mall, we would be busily applying elbow grease—his term for effort—to mowing lawns, scrubbing toilets, making curtains and otherwise engaging in the infinite tasks of home improvement.

To my father, work was as vital to life as breath, and he breathed that spirit into his children. Too bad if some child or other felt sick or tired on a designated workday. "Goldbricker!" he would scold, and though none of us had a clue what a goldbricker was exactly, we knew we had violated our father's primary commandment: Thou shalt not be lazy. . . .

Well into my adulthood, you could find me on any given Saturday on an outside ladder scrubbing windows or inside vacuuming the corner of some closet. Once a friend popped in on a summer afternoon to find me digging into the grooves of a stove knob with a toothpick, trying to remove the greasy gunk. She gave me a sad look.

Mary Schmich
Twentieth century

"What kind of childhood did you have?"

JOHNNY, the kitchen sink has been clogged for days, some
utensil probably fell down there.
And the Drano won't work but smells dangerous, and the
crusty dishes have piled up

waiting for the plumber I still haven't called. This is the
everyday we spoke of.
It's winter again: the sky's a deep headstrong blue, and the
sunlight pours through

the open living room windows because the heat's on too
high in here, and I can't turn it off.
For weeks now, driving, or dropping a bag of groceries in
the street, the bag breaking.

I've been thinking: This is what the living do. And yesterday,
hurrying along those
wobbly bricks in the Cambridge sidewalk, spilling my coffee
down my wrist and sleeve,

I thought it again, and again later, when buying a hairbrush:
This is it.
Parking. Slamming the car door shut in the cold. What you
called *that yearning.*

What you finally gave up. We want the spring to come and
the winter to pass. We want
whoever to call or not call, a letter, a kiss—we want more
and more and then more of it.

But there are moments, walking, when I catch a glimpse of
myself in the window glass,
say, the window of the corner video store, and I'm gripped
by a cherishing so deep

for my own blowing hair, chapped face, and unbuttoned
coat that I'm speechless;
I am living, I remember you.

Marie Howe
Twentieth century

MY father and I are sharing our love
of privacy together, as we often would
when separation was still a window-screen
that could be lifted. A late-April breeze

is in the neighbor's dogwood. The scent
of the dogwood is in the breeze.
So my father hikes up his pant-legs,
plants one knee in dankness, and yanks

a menacing weed. "It's choking my arabis,"
his hands are saying, "so it must be strangled,"
his hands of justice that (thank God)
never fell on me. Kneeling like this,

my father is worshiping again
in the only church he ever trusted.
That's right, Pop, tear away at the earth
you loved. "Each prayer," I tell myself,

"is an act of removal," and wait to learn
what it means. A cardinal, male,
comes down from the sky
to show off his crimson miter.

He's brought his sermon, his *tik-tik, tik-tik,*
along. Praise to that. Praise to grass
for getting stomped on, day after day,
and never once complaining. Praise to names

like "arabis" and "Sisyphus," who my father
is impersonating now, hefting an infant
boulder in the sun. Work: It's all that does,
all that keeps us focused on the real.

Greg Fraser
Twentieth century

MARGARET'S garden is large and lush and colorful, but to name the great variety of flowering and edible stuff that grows there is somehow beside the point. As I see it, the point is this: among the lath and string and climbing vines, among the neat valleys and small green explosions, her hair in a bun, she is intent and precise as a bee. She has a small tool in one hand, a curl of root in the other, she is on her knees, her glasses have ridden out to the edge of her elegant nose, and she is pink with sun, humming.

Gary Gildner
Twentieth century

AFTER hours of picking peaches—
sunstruck—
I lie down in the grass,
don't know where I am.
Asleep in the sun, I wake
as I have for years
to a sense of light
to light
to light in the leaves
of these peach trees.

Margaret Gibson
Twentieth century

IT was afternoon. The trees spread softly, the clouds hung wet and tinted. A buzzard turned a few slow wheels in the sky, and drifted upwards. The dogs promenaded the banks.

"It's time we ate fish," said Virgil.

On a wide sandbar on which seashells lay they dragged up the haul and built a fire.

Then for a long time among clouds of odors and smoke, all half-naked except Doc, they cooked and ate catfish. They ate until the Malones groaned and all the Doyles stretched out on their faces, though for long after, Sam and Robbie Bell sat up to their own little table on a cypress stump and ate on and on. Then they all were silent and still, and one by one fell asleep.

Eudora Welty
Twentieth century

"There ain't a thing better than fish," muttered William Wallace. He lay stretched on his back in the glimmer and shade of trampled sand. His sunburned forehead and cheeks seemed to glow with fire. His eyelids fell. The shadow of a willow branch dipped and moved over him. "There is nothing in the world as good as . . . fish. The fish of Pearl River." Then slowly he smiled. He was asleep.

IT was Saturday and we had been invited to lunch out of a sense of obligation. . . . And there we were, trapped, as if our train had been derailed and we had been forced to settle down among perfect strangers. No one there cared for me and I did not care for them. As for my Saturday—it swayed outside my windows in acacias and shadows. . . .

Only the mistress of the household did not appear to save her Saturday in order to exploit it on a Thursday evening. But how could this woman, whose heart had experienced other Saturdays, have forgotten that people crave more and more? She did not even betray impatience with this heterogeneous gathering in her home, daydreaming and resigned, as if waiting for the next train to leave, any train—rather than remain in that deserted railway station. . . .

We finally moved into the dining room for a lunch without the blessing of hunger. When taken by surprise, we came face to face with the table. This could not be for us. . . .

It was a table prepared for men of good will. Who could the expected guest be who had simply failed to turn up? But it was we ourselves. So that woman served the best no matter the guest? And she was content to wash the feet of the first stranger. We watched, feeling uneasy.

The table had been covered with solemn abundance. Sheaves of wheat were piled up on the white table-cloth. And rosy apples, enormous yellow carrots, round tomatoes with their skins ready to burst, green marrows with translucent skins, pineapples of a malign savageness, oranges golden and tranquil, gherkins bristling like porcupines, cucumbers stretched tight over watery flesh, red, hollow peppers that caused our eyes to smart—were all entangled in moist whiskers of maize, as auburn as if bordering human lips. And the berries of the grape. The purplest of the grapes that could barely wait to be pressed. Nor did they mind who pressed them. The tomatoes were circular for no one: for the atmosphere, for the circular atmosphere. Saturday belonged to anyone who cared to turn up. The oranges would sweeten the tongue of the first person to arrive. Beside the plate of each unwanted guest, the woman who washed the feet of strangers had placed—even without choosing or loving us— a sheaf of wheat, a bunch of fiery radishes, or a crimson slice of water-melon with its merry seeds. All dissected by the Spanish acidity visible in the green lemons. In the earthenware jugs there was milk, as if it had crossed a rocky desert with the goats. Wine that was almost black after being thoroughly trampled shuddered in the clay vessels. Everything was set before us. Everything cleansed of perverse human desire. Everything as it really is, and not as we would wish it to be. Simply existing and intact. Just as a field exists. Just as the mountains exist. Just as man and woman exist, but not those of us who are consumed by greed. Just as Saturday exists. Simply existing. It exists.

On behalf of nothing, it was time to eat. On behalf of no one, it was good. Without any dream. And on a par with day, we gradually became anonymous, growing, rising, to the height of possible existence. Then, like the landed aristocracy, we accepted the table.

Clarice Lispector
Twentieth century

First of all, it begins on Saturday afternoon. In some parts of the country the church bell rings at three o'clock, in others at five o'clock, and the people call it "ringing in the *Feierabend.*" Just as some of the big feasts begin the night before—on Christmas Eve, New Year's Eve, Easter Eve—so every Sunday throughout the year also starts on its eve. That gives Saturday night its hallowed character. When the church bell rings, the people cease working in the fields. They return with the horses and farm machinery, everything is stored away into the barns and sheds, and the barnyard is swept by the youngest farmhand. Then everyone takes "the" bath and the men shave. There is much activity in the

kitchen as the mother prepares part of the Sunday dinner, perhaps a special dessert; the children get a good scrub; everyone gets ready his or her Sunday clothes, and it is usually the custom to put one's room in order—all drawers, cupboards and closets. Throughout the week the meals are usually short and hurried on a farm, but Saturday night everyone takes his time. Leisurely they come strolling to the table, standing around talking and gossiping. After the evening meal the rosary is said. In front of the statue or picture of the Blessed Mother burns a vigil light. After the rosary the father will take a big book containing all the Epistles and Gospels of the Sundays and feast days of the year, and he will read the pertinent ones now to his family. The village people usually go to Confession Saturday night, while the folks from the farms at a distance go on Sunday morning before Mass. Saturday night is a quiet night. There are no parties. People stay at home, getting attuned to Sunday. They go to bed rather early.

Maria Augusta Trapp
Twentieth century

REMEMBERING Jesus' death and resurrection and the coming of the Spirit, Christian Churches from apostolic times would gather on the first day of the week. It was the day of the new creation. It was the "eighth day," the day beyond the world's time. Christians have called it the "Lord's Day."

We have received this tradition. On the Lord's Day we come together, baptized and catechumens alike, to listen to our Scriptures. Then the baptized remain to intercede for all the world, to give God thanks and praise, and to share the Body and Blood of Christ. We prepare for breaking this holy bread by fasting from other food, by remembering our baptism and pondering the Scriptures, and by setting aside a part of our own belongings for the poor and the Church.

Catholic Household
Blessings and Prayers

How do we get there from here? Neglect of the rite of transition is destructive of the whole ritual of the day because we don't change channels like a television set. So, with Sabbath, there needs to be the letting go of the week. . . .

We may move to the Sabbath by a cleaning of the house, by showers and baths which, if even somewhat leisurely, have the power not only to wash the body but to renew it and often to renew the mind also. In those moments of solitary immersion we can mull through and leave behind in the water the cares of the week, matters of work and of money and worry, and so come forth both clean and smiling.

Gabe Huck
Twentieth century

Across the wide waters
    something comes
        floating—a slim
            and delicate

ship, filled
    with white flowers—
        and it moves
            on its miraculous muscles

as though time didn't exist,
    as though bringing such gifts
        to the dry shore
            was a happiness

almost beyond bearing.
    And now it turns its dark eyes,
        it rearranges
            the clouds of its wings,

it trails
    an elaborate webbed foot,
        the color of charcoal.
            Soon it will be here.

Oh, what shall I do
   when that poppy-colored beak
      rests in my hand?
         Said Mrs. Blake of the poet:

I miss my husband's company—
   he is so often
      in paradise.
         Of course! the path to heaven

doesn't lie down in flat miles.
   It's in the imagination
      with which you perceive
         this world,

and the gestures
   with which you honor it.
      Oh, what will I do, what will I say, when those
         white wings
      touch the shore?

Mary Oliver
Twentieth century

W HEN you go to confession on a Saturday night, you go into a warm, dimly lit vastness, with the smell of wax and incense in the air, the smell of burning candles, and if it is a hot summer night there is the sound of a great electric fan, and the noise of the streets coming in to emphasize the stillness. There is another sound too, besides that of the quiet movements of the people from pew to confession to altar rail; there is the sliding of the shutters of the little window between you and the priest in his "box."

Dorothy Day
Twentieth century

A scarf trailing
over the lilac sunset,
fair weather clouds,
cirrus uncinus
silk chiffon.
Twilight softens the air,
whispering, come,
lie down with me.

Untie the knots of the will.
Loosen
your clenched grip
barren hills of bone.
Here, no edges to hone,
only the palm fallen
open as a rose about
to toss its petals.

What you have made,
what you have spoiled
let go.
Let twilight empty
the crowned rooms
quiet the jostling colors
to hues of swirling water
pearls of fog.

This is the time
for letting time go
like a released balloon
dwindling.
Tilt your neck and let
your face open to the sky
like a pond catching light
drinking the darkness.

Marge Piercy
Twentieth century

Whosoever would keep the Lord's Day,
Even would it be to him and lasting,
From setting of sun on Saturday
Till rising of sun on Monday.

Celtic poem

The old, wise Sabbath says: *Stop now.* As the sun touches the horizon, take the hand off the plow, put down the phone, let the pen rest on the paper, turn off the computer, leave the mop in the bucket and the car in the drive. There is no room for negotiation, no time to be seduced by the urgency of our responsibilities. We stop because there are forces larger than we that take care of the universe, and while our efforts are important, necessary, and useful, they are not (nor are we) indispensable. The galaxy will somehow manage without us for this hour, this day, and so we are invited—nay, commanded—to relax, and enjoy our relative unimportance, our humble place at the table in a very large world. The deep wisdom embedded in creation will take care of things for while.

Wayne Muller
Twentieth century

Don't surrender your loneliness
So quickly.
Let it cut more deep.

Let it ferment and season you
As few human
Or even divine ingredients can.

Something missing in my heart tonight
Has made my eyes so soft,
My voice
So tender,

My need of God
Absolutely
Clear.

Hafiz
Fourteenth century

GOD in heaven,
Let me really feel my nothingness,
Not in order to despair over it,
But in order to feel the more powerfully
The greatness of your goodness.

*Søren Kierkegaard
Nineteenth century*

O God our King, by the resurrection of your Son Jesus
Christ on the first day of the week, you conquered sin,
put death to flight, and gave us the hope of everlasting life:
Redeem all our days by this victory; forgive our sins, banish
our fears, make us bold to praise you and to do your will;
and steel us to wait for the consummation of your kingdom
on the last great Day; through the same Jesus Christ our Lord.

*Prayers for Pastor
and People*

ALL of us, gathered in Your holy house
stand (unworthy as we are)
and send up to You our evening hymn,
O Christ our God,
and call upon You from the depths
to deliver Your people from the grasp of the Adversary,
O Christ who in Your infinite love for Your people
has enlightened the world
by Your Resurrection on the third day.

Byzantine liturgy

ON Saturday evening, when the vigil for Sunday began,
the faithful were accustomed to gather for an evening
of prayer; this service was called the Lucernary. A lamp was
lit to commemorate the risen Christ, who is the splendid . . .
parousia. It is this ancient office, which had become a daily
evening prayer for the entire Christian community, that
Hippolytus describes:

When evening comes and the bishop has arrived, the deacon brings a lamp. Standing in the midst of the faithful, the bishop gives thanks; he begins with the greeting:

> The Lord be with you!
> And all the people answer:
>> And with your spirit!
>> —Let us give thanks to the Lord.
> They will answer:
>> It is right and just.
>> His are greatness and magnificence
>> as well as glory.

He is not to say: "Let us lift up our hearts," because this is to be said at the moment of the offering.

Then let him pray like this:

> We give you thanks, O God,
> through your Son, Jesus Christ, our Lord,
> for having enlightened us
> by revealing to us the incorruptible light.
> Having ended the course of this day
> and reached the edge of the night,
> having been filled by the light of day
> which you created for our joy,
> we now possess, through your kindness,
> the evening light.
> Therefore do we praise you and glorify you
> through your Son, Jesus Christ, our Lord.

> Through him be glory yours, power and honor,
> with the Holy Spirit, now and always
> and for ever and ever.

Lucien Deiss,
Twentieth century
(quoting Hippolytus,
Third century)

Then all are to answer: "Amen."
After the meal they will rise for prayer. The children will sing psalms, as well as the virgins.

WE offer up to You our evening worship,
O uncreated Light,
who were, and are, and are to come!
For through the flesh as in a glass
You have shone upon the world,
descending even into hell,
setting free those in darkness there,
and showing forth to all the world
the light of the Resurrection:
Glory to You, O Lord, O Giver of light!

Byzantine liturgy

I try to ignore the stars, a billion witnesses
that I give myself to black skies, not even gravity holding
me back, cast into outer darkness. Not stars always on fire,
not fire,

but beyond, whatever scattered them: *that* power.

Walt McDonald
Twentieth century

O Brightness of the immortal Father's face,
Most holy, heav'nly, blest, Lord Jesus
Christ, in whom His truth and grace
Are visibly expressed.

The sun is setting now, and one by one
The lamps of evening shine;
We praise the eternal Father, and the Son,
And Spirit Blest, divine.

Forever are you worthy to receive
Our thankful praises, Lord.
O Son of God, our joy, in whom we live,
Adored through all the world.

Phos Hilaron
Second–Third century

O most
wretched and blind, come home!
    Where love has been
burns the great lantern of the Holy Ghost.
Here in His light; review your world of frost:
a drifting miracle! What had been night
reels with unending eucharists of light.

Jessica Powers
Twentieth century

S OMEONE has left a light on at the boathouse
to guide the fishermen back after dark.
The light makes no sound as it comes.
It flies over the waves like a bird with one wing.
Its path is a boatful of the dead, trying to return to life
over the broken waters.

                    And the light
simply comes, bearing no gifts,
as if the camels had arrived without the Wise Men.
It is steady, holding us to our old mountain home.
Now as we watch the moon rises over the popple forest.
It too arrives without fuss,
it goes between the boards around the pulp-cutter's house—
the same fence we pass through by opening the gate.

Robert Bly
Twentieth century

J ESUS whom I look at shrouded here below,
I beseech you send me what I thirst for so,
Some day to gaze on you face to face in light
And be blest for ever with your glory's sight.

Latin prayer
Thirteenth century

A PART from the celebration of the Eucharist, the oldest of the Sunday services is the vigil. This assembly for prayer during the final hours of Saturday night is attested in the East, and especially in Jerusalem, in the fourth century; the Frankish councils of the sixth to the ninth centuries make frequent reference to it, but Rome was never to have it. On the other hand, at Rome the two sacred vigils for Easter Sunday and Pentecost Sunday and the vigils for the Ember Days used to begin on Saturday evening and continue to morning.

P. Jounel
Twentieth century

W HEN servants are waiting for their masters to return from a banquet they need to stay awake all night, awaiting his arrival: their *loins should be girded* and their *lamps lighted* (Luke 12:35); they cannot allow themselves to drop off into deep sleep, seeing that they do not know whether their master will be returning that evening, or in the middle of the night, or at cock-crow (cf. Luke 12:38), or the next morning; they are afraid he may suddenly come and find them asleep. We too, then, should be wakeful and prepared, just as our Lord bade us: *You too should be prepared, for the Son of Man will come at a moment when you are not expecting him* (Matthew 24:44).

This applies particularly to the holy day of Sunday, the great day of the Resurrection on which we expect our King to return from on high to take us off to the wedding feast he has prepared for us. We should especially display our eager readiness by our wakefulness in singing psalms and in praying during the long vigil that lasts the entire night, after the example that our Lord taught us when he went up alone to the mountain, watching without sleep the whole night in prayer to God (cf. Luke 6:12).

Martyrius (Sahdona)
Seventh century

IT was also said of him [Abba Arsenius] that on Saturday evenings, if preparing for the glory of Sunday, he would turn his back on the sun and stretch out his hands in prayer towards the heavens, till once again the sun shone on his face. Then he would sit down.

ONE of the first depictions of Christ in art known to us comes from a Roman mausoleum mosaic discovered in the excavations under the Vatican basilica. In a ceiling of gold a lush grapevine turns and curls. At its center is the sun chariot and the four horses of Apollo (Helios to the Greeks). The driver is a young beardless white-robed man whose head stands out against the background of the sun. In the midst of the sunburst, however, is the cross. This is Christos-Helios, Christ the Sun of Justice. This is the Christ we greet when at the lamplighting hour we sing "Jesus Christ is the Light of the world. A Light no darkness can extinguish." This is the true and everlasting Prometheus who brought us fire not stolen but rightfully his own, who died not in punishment for the fire given but to show us how the fire could consume for the life of the world. The myth lives on but is transformed.

Andrew D. Ciferni
Twentieth century

IT was already night and some of the people were keeping vigil in anticipation of the synaxis, when suddenly the general Syrianus appeared with more than 5,000 soldiers, heavily armed with bared swords, bows and arrows, and cudgels, as I said above. He surrounded the church, stationing his soldiers closely together, so that no one could leave the church and slip by them. Now it seemed to me unreasonable to leave the people in such confusion and not rather to bear the brunt of battle for them, so sitting upon the throne, I urged the deacon to read a psalm and the people to respond, "For his mercy endureth forever" (Psalm 135:1).

Athanasius
Fourth century

Out of the depths I cry to you, O Lord.
   Lord, hear my voice!
Let your ears be attentive
   to the voice of my supplications!

If you, O Lord, should mark iniquities,
   Lord, who could stand?
But there is forgiveness with you,
   so that you may be revered.

I wait for the Lord, my soul waits,
   and in his word I hope;
my soul waits for the Lord
   more than those who watch for the morning,
   more than those who watch for the morning.

O Israel, hope in the Lord!
   For with the Lord there is steadfast love,
   and with him is great power to redeem.   Psalm 130:1–7

O God, the source of eternal light: Shed forth your unending day upon us who watch for you, that our lips may praise you, our lives may bless you, and our worship on the morrow give you glory; through Jesus Christ our Lord.

The Book of Common Prayer

THEN the prophet Miriam, Aaron's sister, took a tambourine in her hand; and all the women went out after her with tambourines and with dancing.

Exodus 15:20

THESE were the years of CYO (Catholic Youth Organization) dances, where I would stand with other like-minded fourteen- and fifteen-year-old boys, close to the wall, as if unconsciously hankering for protection from something, while out in the middle of the dance floor the girls were busy bopping, twisting, jitter-bugging, and generally having a good time.

We boys stood rigidly, arms folded, feet riveted to the floor, while the girls giggled and glided, seeming to pay us little if any attention.

I do not know much of the home lives of those other adolescent boys, but there was something curious about my time at home that did not quite match my behavior at the dances.

At home, atop the oval hooked rug and in front of the cathode ray image of Buddy Deane that flickered across the Muntz, my sisters had taught me to dance. The twins, a year older and many years wiser, out of the goodness of their hearts or possibly the need for a partner with a little testosterone, had initiated me into the mysteries of the bop and the slow dance.

Three or four afternoons a week we would glide, stomp, and twirl until Buddy gave way to Rocky and Bullwinkle. . . . When the weekend rolled around, however, the good times did not roll with it. I always assumed my place amidst the wall liners whose conversation inevitably turned to how there weren't any girls worth dancing with anyway. The truth of the matter, of course, was not so simple. In those skinny human frames dabbed with too much English Leather, the fear of ridicule had somehow married the most delicate kind of machismo to produce a predictable inaction—an inaction born in early adolescence and not so easily lost. There was a simple human law at work among the wall liners: doing nothing can produce no pain; nothing ventured, nothing lost.

Stephen Vicchio
Twentieth century

Tɪᴍ . . . went quietly downstairs and stood on the terrace and watched the evening sun making the rocks move, making them breathe, very quietly expand and contract like some organism under the sea. He thought, well, something has happened *now* which can't unhappen. And yet at any moment—He did not want to think frightening thoughts. He felt a blank blinding empty happiness. He also felt extremely hungry. He wanted to dance. He went down onto the flowery lawn and executed a few Morris steps. Then with his hands on his hips he danced down as far as the olive grove. He stood there and gazed at the rocks. When he turned about he saw that Gertrude was standing on the terraces in a flimsy white garment which might have been a nightdress. He began to dance towards her across the flower-shadowed grass.

Gertrude, as if she could hear the same silent music, came down the steps and joined in the dance. Instinctively, hands on hips, they danced with the zigzag snakelike motion of a hay. It was as if other dancers were present to whom, as they passed, they turned their backs until, in the middle of the meadow, solemnly, unsmilingly, they passed each other, reached the extremities of the space and came weaving back. Gertrude's small bare feet flashed among the blue flowers and it was toward her swift feet that Tim looked each time as he approached her. At last the music ceased, the dance was done, they slowed down and in the centre of the meadow took hands and smiled.

Iris Murdoch
Twentieth century

Mᴀʀɢᴀʀᴇᴛ likes to dance. She likes to fix herself up—high heels, seamed hose, a peach-colored silk dress—and drive over to Eugene, to a cowboy bar we found. We dance to Hank Williams and Webb Pierce and when the band takes a break we put quarters in the jukebox and dance to Patsy Cline and Tammy Wynette. I have purchased proper tack for these nights, a Stetson and a pair of Tony Lama boots, and I know "I'm Walkin' the Floor Over You," by the great Ernest Tubb, by heart. The silk dress Margaret wears belonged to her mother. It has padded shoulders,

Gary Gildner
Twentieth century

a tight waist, and falls sleekly to her knees. . . . She's a shimmering knockout, a perfect reproduction from the '40s. She keeps her glasses in her purse and her eyes sparkle.

I could take the Harlem night
and wrap around you,
Take the neon lights and make a crown,
Take the Lenox Avenue busses,
Taxis, subways,
And for your love song tone their rumble down.
Take Harlem's heartbeat,
Make a drumbeat,
Put it on a record, let it whirl,
And while we listen to it play,
Dance with you till day—
Dance with you, my sweet brown Harlem girl.

Langston Hughes
Twentieth century

SUNDAYS too my father got up early
and put his clothes on in the blueblack cold,
then with cracked hands that ached
from labor in the weekday weather made
banked fires blaze. No one ever thanked him.

I'd wake and hear the cold splintering, breaking.
When the rooms were warm, he'd call,
and slowly I would rise and dress,
fearing the chronic angers of that house,

Speaking indifferently to him,
who had driven out the cold
and polished my good shoes as well.
What did I know, what did I know
of love's austere and lonely offices?

Robert Hayden
Twentieth century

THIS is the day of light:
Let there be light today;
O Dayspring, rise up on our night,
And chase its gloom away.

This is the day of rest:
Our failing strength renew;
On weary brain and troubled breast
Shed Thou Thy fresh'ning dew.

This is the day of peace:
Thy peace our spirits fill;
Bid Thou the blasts of discord cease,
The waves of strife be still.

This is the day of pray'r:
Let earth to heav'n draw near;
Lift up our hearts to seek Thee there,
Come down to meet us here.

This is the first day of days:
Send forth Thy quick'ning breath,
And wake dead souls to love and praise,
O Vanquisher of death!

John Ellerton
Nineteenth century

IT is a beauteous morning, calm and free.
   The fairways sparkle. Gleam the shaven grasses.
Mirth fills the locker rooms and, hastily,
   Stewards fetch ice, fresh towels, and extra glasses.
On terraces the sandaled women freshen
   Their lipstick; gather to gossip, poised and cool;
And the shrill adolescent takes possession,
   Plunging and splashing, of the swimming pool.

It is a beauteous morn, opinion grants.
   Nothing remains of last night's Summer Formal
Save palms and streamers and the wifely glance,
   Directed with more watchfulness than normal,
At listless mate who tugs his necktie loose,
Moans, shuns the light, and gulps tomato juice.

Phyllis McGinley
Twentieth century

JOHN Vianney, the parish priest of Ars, . . . devoted much of his early pastorate to drying out his wine-soaked farmers so that they would be able to so much as get up for Sunday mass. The crossroads taverns had all the best of it. *Monsieur l'abbé* was a spoilsport, a fanatic because . . . he thought that Jesus was the son of man and lord of the Sabbath.

Gerard Sloyan
Twentieth century

Fʀᴏᴍ the Appalachian Mountains to the Rocky Mountains, there is a vast area where people don't have repeated contact with people of color, who get their opinions and beliefs from what they see on television. And that's not the way of the world. . . .

. . . Look at the Sunday morning news shows. . . . Around 95 percent of their guests are white, yet people of color read the news, report the news, and make the news. Dr. King used to say that 11 o'clock on Sunday morning was the most segregated hour in America. . . .

He was talking about the churches, but I would dare say it's the same case with respect to these talking-head shows.

Kweisi Mfume
Twentieth century

Cᴏᴍᴘʟᴀᴄᴇɴᴄɪᴇs of the peignoir, and late
Coffee and oranges in a sunny chair,
And the green freedom of a cockatoo
Upon a rug mingle to dissipate
The holy hush of ancient sacrifice.
She dreams a little, and she feels the dark
Encroachment of that old catastrophe,
As a calm darkens among water-lights.
The pungent oranges and bright, green wings
Seem things in some procession of the dead,
Winding across wide water, without sound.
The day is like wide water, without sound,
Stilled for the passing of her dreaming feet
Over the seas, to silent Palestine,
Dominion of the blood and sepulchre.

Wallace Stevens
Twentieth century

Yᴏᴜ rose from the dead, O Life of all, and a resplendent angel cried out to the women: stop your tears and inform the apostles. Cry out in praise that Christ the Lord is risen, being pleased as God to save human race.

Orthodox liturgy

O come and let us worship Christ!
All people, bow before him
Who from the dead a Victor rose:
Sing praises and adore him
The stone was sealed up on the tomb,
And soldiers guard were keeping,
Where in the cold embrace of death
The Christ of God was sleeping

The morning star shone in the east,
The hills with light were glowing;
The Christ arose, upon the world
His light and life bestowing

Wherefore from highest heav'n the hosts
Their songs of vict'ry blending,
Give glory to the mighty Lord,
And sing his reign unending

John Brownlie
Twentieth century

OVER the water of the world again
the Spirit broods;
Over the chaos the minds of all
and down the dream-deserted solitudes.

I know His ominous presence, and I hear
His prophecy of flight
over a world of thought at the first clear
and thunderous dismissal of the night.

How shall that burst of radiance be greeted
as, from the black abyss
the first day wakens when it hears repeated
that cry to light, torn out of Genesis?

Jessica Powers
Twentieth century

TRANSCENDENT God in whom we live
The Resurrection and the Light;
We sing for you a morning hymn
To end the silence of the night.

When early cock begins to crow
And everything from sleep awakes,
New life and hope spring up again
While out of darkness colour breaks.

Creator of all things that are,
The measure and the end of all,
Forgiving God, forget our sins
And hear our prayer before we call.

Praise Father, Son and Holy Ghost,
Blest Trinity and source of grace,
Who call us forth from nothingness
To find in you our resting-place.

*The Stanbrook
Abbey Hymnal*

SUNDAY morning, 5 AM. First light touches the tops of trees, and in the muddy parking lot of the bar west of town a bride leans into the window of a car, talking to a couple inside. She holds her veil in her hands. A late-model pickup, louder than it has to be, roars into the lot. Three young men get out, one still in his rented tux—and cowboy hat, of course. They drop their beer cans into a pile. A wedding in the West.

I keep moving and don't stare. Walking near dawn on summer mornings I often pass by cars and pickups parked along the old highway, hung over and half-dressed people stirring inside; people who most likely don't want to be seen, let alone greeted cheerfully in the light of dawn.

I don't care who they are; and even if I knew, I wouldn't tell. They might not believe that; this is a small town. But sex is a mystery, like faith, or love, and deserves to have the glow of silence around it.

I've been asked to preach this morning and am thinking about my sermon. The wind comes up with dawn: two mule deer, a male and a female, cross the highway just a hundred feet in front of me, and run off into a hayfield. The wideness of God's mercy, as the old hymn says; the sudden way that grace makes all things good.

Kathleen Norris
Twentieth century

IT is good to give thanks to the LORD,
    to sing praises to your name, O Most High;
to declare your steadfast love in the morning,
    and your faithfulness by night,
to the music of the lute and the harp,
    to the melody of the lyre.
For you, O LORD, have made me glad by your work;
    at the works of your hands I sing for joy.

Psalm 92:1–4

THIS is a day of new beginnings,
    time to remember, and move on,
time to believe what love is bringing,
laying to rest the pain that's gone.

For by the life and death of Jesus,
love's mighty Spirit, now as then,
can make for us a world of difference
as faith and hope are born again.

Then let us, with the Spirit's daring,
step from the past, and leave behind
our disappointment, guilt and grieving,
seeking new paths, and sure to find.

Christ is alive, and goes before us
to show and share what love can do.
This is a day of new beginnings;
our God is making all things new.

In faith we'll gather 'round the table
to show and share what love can do.
This is a day of new beginnings;
our God is making all things new.

Brian Wren
Twentieth century

WHEN you tasted death in the flesh, O Lord, you checked the bitterness of death by your resurrection and strengthened us, restoring victory over the old curse. Therefore, O Lord, defender of our life, glory to you.

Orthodox liturgy

HOW does faith come—like a hummingbird darting by— or a pair of elk cows clipping our grass at dawn, sniffing the picnic table while we wait
with the blinds raised. Soon, beams will splash
the mountain peak, lights will come on,

a cabin door will close, the elk will lift their heads
and stare, and trot with eyes wide back to the tree line.
But suddenly, others come, almost glowing in their blond,
thick, winter coats, bowing to grass we've watered
and not mowed, hoping for this moment—four,

fourteen, the whole herd here on our lawn,
sisters and mothers on our green slope,
cougars and coyotes a thousand yards behind them,
calves on their way within weeks—but all that's later,
and the best grass since last summer is right now.

Walt McDonald
Twentieth century

WHEN Mama opened her eyes early the next morning, bright sunshine flooded the bedroom. It took her a moment to remember she was back in Sweden, in the parsonage. She rubbed her eyes and looked over at Pontus sleeping heavily beside her. The quilt, rising and falling gently with his breathing, covered half his face. Mama peeked at the clock. There was still half an hour before she had to get up and start the coffee. She settled back for a few more winks. Suddenly she remembered. Why, this was *Sunday* morning and she was a married woman now! Mama almost chuckled aloud. Would Pontus remember, too, that a husband was supposed to bring his *wife* coffee on Sunday morning? For years as a housekeeper she had brought Pontus coffee *every* morning. On weekdays she had used the brightly painted wooden tray; but on Sundays she had carried the silver tray with a very special coffeepot and Papa's favorite *vienerbröd.* She would knock softly at his door, then wait for his sleepy voice to answer before she entered.

Now she glanced over at him again, sleeping so soundly. What if he didn't wake up in time to bring *her* coffee? Well— she better make sure that he did. Cautiously, she touched his leg with her toe. Papa slept on. She "touched" a little harder. This time he stirred and threw back the quilt from his face.

"Pontus," she whispered softly. "It's morning—our *first* morning in the parsonage."

"So it is—so it is." Pontus stretched luxuriously. "And our first *coffee,* too. It will taste good, Maria."

Mama's heart sank. He *had* forgotten. But there was still time if only she could think what to say.

"It's Sunday, Pontus," she ventured.

"Well?"

Mama settled back against her pillow and closed her eyes pretending to be sleepy. "Don't you remember what husbands do on Sunday, Pontus *lilla?*"

Papa sat up suddenly and stared at her without speaking.

"This is *my* day, Pontus," Mama murmured sleepily. "You are to bring *me* coffee this morning."

Papa pushed back the quilt reluctantly and threw his legs over the side of the bed. "Of course, Maria, I never thought of it," he said, and started for the kitchen.

Mama smiled as she watched him. He looked so funny in that nightshirt, with his carpet slippers flapping. But she loved him so much. She was glad she had made everything ready in the kitchen the night before. The *tyre-wood* lay beside the stove, along with the exact amount of regular wood needed to make the coffee boil. (Pontus had always been very particular about how much wood she used; and only enough *tyre-wood* to make sure the regular wood caught fire quickly.) She had filled the coffeepot last night, too, and measured out the right amount of coffee. Even the tray had been prepared—the big silver one, for she had completely forgotten that *she* was the one who would be honored.

Mama snuggled into her pillow and waited. Presently Papa pushed open the bedroom door. The coffee smelled so good. Maria sat up brushing back her hair from her face. "You are a real husband, now, Pontus," she cried.

Thyra Ferré Bjorn
Twentieth century

CHRISTIANITY has given us . . . the Sabbath, the jubilee of the whole world, whose light dawns welcome alike into the closet of the philosopher, into the garret of toil, and into prison-cells, and everywhere suggests, even to the vile, the dignity of spiritual being. Let it stand forevermore, a temple, which new love, new faith, new sight shall restore to more than its first splendor to mankind.

Ralph Waldo Emerson
Nineteenth century

THEN she got up from the chair where she had been dozing, and went, half-asleep, to the window to assure herself that morning was at hand. The streets were unusually quiet with a Sabbath stillness. No factory bells that morning; no early workmen going to their labours; no slip-shod girls cleaning the windows of the little shops which broke the monotony of the street; instead, you might see here and there some operative sallying forth for a breath of country air, or some father leading out his wee toddling bairns for the unwonted pleasure of a walk with 'Daddy,' in the clear

Elizabeth Gaskell
Nineteenth century

frosty morning. Men with more leisure on week-days would perhaps have walked quicker than they did through the fresh sharp air of this Sunday morning; but to them there was a pleasure, and absolute refreshment in the dawdling gait they, one and all of them, had.

Maronite liturgy

B LESSED be he who has raised the great day of Sunday above all other days. The heavens and the earth, angels and people give themselves over to joy.

O H, the Genoa salami and the prosciutto and the bread, hot from the ovens of Lanzone, the baker down the block! And the glory of the fresh fruit! Cherries, peaches, tart Italian prunes. I tell you, nothing Omar Khayyám ever wrote taught me more about the delights of the food God lets us eat than did my father's store.

And to have this food at the beach on Sunday mornings! Because, finally, my father decided he could afford the luxury of a single morning a week—on Sundays, of course—to take the family out. Imagine being nine or ten years old and having this food in the summer, at the ocean, sitting on the clean, white sand of the beautiful beaches of Long Island or on the sweet, clean grass of the beautiful parks of Queens County. My father would bite a piece of grass or splash us with a handful of the Atlantic Ocean and say to us, "You see, kids, the beautiful things that God has made."

Mario Cuomo
Twentieth century

A FTER a special breakfast, our house falls into *silence* for an hour. Each family member goes to his/her room or to some other place alone. It is the only waking hour in the week when the house is silent: you can feel the stillness opening and inviting a reflective mind sensitive to the hidden Spirit among us.

The primary guideline for the hour is that we be present to life as a gift from and in the Lord. For very young children such an hour is not likely to be possible. Older ones, though, are capable of such quiet things as reading, writing, and drawing for an hour. We encourage them just to let something spontaneous flow through them if they write or draw, and to be thankfully aware of God's love for them and for the way that love comes through everything around them that they see and enjoy, even sometimes through what is painful. Occasionally our children like to spend part of the time staring at the wonders of the underwater world in their fish tanks. . . .

It is our own prayer, reading, silence, rest, and appreciative presence to this giftedness of life in Christ that we feed into corporate worship. This is the spacious bed that sets off liturgy and lets it radiate among us. No great dramatic liturgy or sermon is needed to force-feed the Gospel into people's scattered minds. A proper Sabbath setting brings its own attunement to the Word and Sacrament. The slightest, simplest sound, word, sight can then set off a holy resonance within and among us. This is why the simplest liturgy is experienced so fully in the midst of a retreat, when we have ordered Sabbath time together.

Tilden Edwards
Twentieth century

I N houses and apartments all through the neighborhood, the true entrance procession of this Mass has been in full swing, sometimes hectic. Sunday clothes are being put on. Many families are finishing breakfast, conscious of the one-hour fast. Here and there are adults who choose to fast altogether until taking Holy Communion. Some households make a conscious effort to keep the morning quiet: no radio or television, and the Sunday papers wait until later in the day.

In a surprisingly large number of households, but still a tiny minority, the Sunday Scriptures have already been read aloud together on Friday or Saturday evening. Others met during the week in Spanish-speaking or English-speaking prayer groups where the Lectionary's Sunday readings were pondered. Teenagers spent part of the regular youth group meeting reading these Scriptures.

The liturgy is the work of the whole assembly, and here we begin to see that many take this seriously. Many have prepared themselves to come together today and participate fully in this Eucharist.

So this is the entrance procession, coming from all directions, made up of all ages, several races, a variety of economic circumstances and political outlooks—and speaking at least three first languages! But they are all in a great procession, the Church assembling in the house of the Church. "We shall go up with joy," "Que alegría cuando me dijeron vamos a la casa del Señor," or as we used to pray from Psalm 43, "Introibo ad altare Dei."

Cardinal Roger
Mahony
Twentieth century

WE pray you, Father of the only-begotten Son,
Lord of all things,
Creator of the created world,
Author of what exists.

Our pure hands
we hold out toward you;
and our spirits
we raise toward you,

We pray your mercy,
your pity and your goodness;
amend us, increase in us
power, faith, and knowledge.

Cast your eyes on us, Lord,
we lay our weaknesses before you.
Grant pardon and mercy to us all.
Have mercy on your people,
show them your goodness,
make them generous, chaste, and pure.

Send the angelic spirits
that your entire people
may be holy and unspotted.

We pray you,
send your Holy Spirit into our souls.
Grant us to understand
the Scriptures that be inspired,
to interpret them clearly and worthily,
so that all the people here present
may draw profit from them,

Through you only-begotten Son, Jesus Christ,
in the Holy Spirit.
Through him, glory to you and power,
now and for ever and ever!

Serapion of Thmuis
Fourth century

SOME keep the Sabbath going to Church—
I keep it, staying at Home—
With a Bobolink for a Chorister—
And an Orchard, for a Dome—

Some keep the Sabbath in Surplice—
I just wear my Wings—
And instead of tolling the Bell, for Church,
Our little Sexton—sings.

God preaches, a noted Clergyman—
And the sermon is never long,
So instead of getting to Heaven, at last—
I'm going, all along.

Emily Dickinson
Nineteenth century

WHEN you are teaching, command and exhort the people to be faithful to the assembly of the church. Let them not fail to attend, but let them gather faithfully together. Let no one deprive the Church by staying away; if they do, they deprive the body of Christ of one of its members!

For you must not think only of others but of yourself as well, when you hear the words that our Lord spoke: "Who does not gather with me, scatters" (Matthew 12:30). Since you are the members of Christ, you must not scatter yourselves outside the Church by failing to assemble there. For we have Christ for our Head, as he himself promised and announced, so that "you have become sharers with us."

Do not, then, make light of your own selves, do not deprive our Savior of his members, do not rend, do not scatter his Body!

The Didascalia
of the Apostles
Second century

MOST glorious Lord of life, that on this day
    Didst make thy triumph over death and sin;
And having harrowed hell didst bring away
Captivity thence captive, us to win:
This joyous day, dear Lord, with joy begin,
    And grant that we for whom thou didest die
    Being with thy dear blood clean washed from sin,
    May live forever in felicity.

And that thy love we weighing worthily,
    May likewise love thee for the same again;
    And for thy sake that all like dear didst buy,
    With love may one another entertain.
So let us love, dear love, like as we ought.
Love is the lesson which the Lord us taught.

Edmund Spenser
Sixteenth century

GREAT grandmother in dacron brocade suit,
snowflake prayer cap, props her spiral spine
hymnal on the altar rail and raising
her lace hanky, prompts the early arrivers
to join in: "Go tell it on the mountain,
over the hills . . ." The congregation rises
in response, rolling their rich lyrics
over the double glass storm doors, down
the gravel path of parked cars into
the fallen winter cornstalks.

A stack of tambourines rests on the aisle
end of each white pine pew of the Morning
Star Hill Pentecostal. When the guitar
and piano strike introductory chords,
cousins in bows and cornrows rock
the bench, bat-jingle bat-jingle-bam.
On Daddy's lap, Baby Elizabeth lifts
this instrument in her one-year-old arms,
and with perfect fingers she tap-taps
slowly, slowly, the silver circle bangles.

Chris Llewellyn
Twentieth century

SAFELY through another week
God has brought us on our way;
Let us now a blessing seek,
Waiting in his courts today:
Day of all the week the best,
Emblem of eternal rest.

John Newton
Nineteenth century

THOSE who have received the grace of baptism are not
saved as individuals alone, but as members of the mystical body, having become part of the People of God. It is
important therefore that they come together to express fully

the very identity of the church, the *ekklesia,* the assembly called together by the Risen Lord who offered his life "to reunite the scattered children of God" (John 11:52). They have become one in Christ (cf. Galatians 3:28) through the gift of the Spirit. This unity becomes visible when Christians gather together: It is then that they come to know vividly and to testify to the world that they are the people redeemed, drawn "from every tribe and language and people and nation" (Revelation 5:9). The assembly of Christ's disciples embodies from age to age the image of the first Christian community, which Luke gives as an example in the Acts of the Apostles when he recounts that the first baptized believers "devoted themselves to the apostles' teaching and fellowship, to the breaking of bread and the prayers" (2:42).

Pope John Paul II
Twentieth century

O N the way to [the] altar of God, most of [the] people pass by the large Baptismal Font and take water from it, perhaps remembering their own Baptism. They enter their liturgy marked with the water of Baptism, marked with the cross of Christ whose Body we became in those waters (CCC: 1267).

At 9:45 the choir is assembled and a brief but serious rehearsal begins, firming up what was practiced last Wednesday evening. . . . By now the presider is vested and stands with servers and lectors near the main entrance, adding to the welcome of the ushers. The ushers, knowing the church will be full, are doing their best to fill the pews nearest the altar first. They make special efforts to see that parents with very small infants get places in the first rows (where there are more comfortable chairs).

Likewise, the ushers invited any who would find the communion procession difficult to take places in those areas throughout the assembly space with room for wheelchairs. . . . The sacristan has invited the gift-bearers to bring the bread and wine forward at the proper time and is now going over the "checklist for Sunday Mass" before joining the assembly. Sponsors and catechumens find each other and fill in the first few rows of one section of the church.

Although people go out of their way to greet one another
and be gracious, it is never done in such a way that you
feel one person is the host and another is the guest. Everyone
is at home.

Cardinal Roger
Mahony
Twentieth century

PRAISE the LORD, all you nations!
      Extol him, all you peoples!
For great is his steadfast love toward us,
    and the faithfulness of the LORD endures forever.
Praise the LORD!

Psalm 117

THIS principle of one common celebration, accepted and
put into practice every Sunday till the threshold of modern times, and still realized in many country parishes, brings
to light an element which belongs in every genuine celebration: *assembly.* A person can do an hour of meditation, of
interior recollection, all by himself and on his own account,
in the privacy of his own room or in some quiet corner of a
church; but he can *celebrate* only together with others of a
like mind. Celebration is the expression of thought or joy or
enthusiasm communally shared. Celebration demands the
resonance of one and the same thought or mood in many
minds. And human nature requires such resonance. It cannot be satisfied by quiet alone, nor even solely with interior
recollection; it needs also celebration.

Josef A. Jungmann
Twentieth century

WITH a clamor of bells that set the swallows soaring,
the Festival of Summer came to the city Omelas,
bright-towered by the sea. The rigging of the boats in harbor sparkled with flags. In the streets between houses with
red roofs and painted walls, between old moss-grown gar-
dens and under avenues of trees, past great parks and public buildings, processions moved. Some were decorous: old

people in long stiff robes of mauve and grey, grave master workmen, quiet, merry women carrying their babies and chatting as they walked. In other streets the music beat faster, a shimmering of gong and tambourine, and the people went dancing, the procession was a dance. Children dodged in and out, their high calls rising like the swallows' crossing flights over the music and the singing.

Joyous! How is one to tell about joy? How describe the citizens of Omelas?

Ursula K. LeGuin
Twentieth century

THE venerable old man used to say that the entrance of the people into the church with the bishop represents the conversion of the unfaithful from faithlessness to faith and from sin and error to the recognition of God as well as the passage of the faithful from vice and ignorance to virtue and knowledge. For entrance into the church signifies not only the conversion of infidels to the true and only God but also the amendment of each one of us who believe but who yet violate the Lord's commandments. . . . When someone is entangled in any kind of vice but should cease voluntarily to be held by its attention and deliberately to act according to it and changes his life for the better by preferring virtue to vice, such a person can be properly and truly considered and spoken of as entering with Christ our God and High Priest into virtue, which is the church understood figuratively.

Maximus the
Confessor
Seventh century

COME Sunday, Mommy wakes me up with whispers.
LaTasha, honey, she says to me.
Time to shed dawn's cozy quilt.
Come on, Sweet Pea. Open up those eyes.

I rise and wander to the kitchen,
where Mommy makes my hair and scalp
tingle with oil and comb and brush.
If only she didn't weave the braids so tight.

I fight to keep from squirming round
until the braiding's finally done,
'cause once I'm dressed, I look so nice,
I practically run to Paradise—
     to Paradise Baptist Church.

Nikki Grimes
Twentieth century

THE door of the little white church was propped open when they arrived, and members of the congregation were waving fans of leaves and paper to relieve the stuffiness inside. Fair Annie and her brothers and sisters took their places on the choir benches; they accounted for almost half of the group. Then Otis came in and sat down beside her. When he smiled at her in his special way, she was ready to forgive him for last night and to think up excuses for his behavior: Patty Ruth Ann's city clothes and wily ways had been too much for him. It wasn't his fault.

While waiting for the preacher to arrive, the choir warmed up with "When We Get to Heaven." Fair Annie sang joyously as her discontent faded away. Everything was right with the world again; things were just the way they were supposed to be. The folks who'd been saved sat at the front of the church, and those who had yet to be "called" sat in the back. And outside, the usual bunch of husbands and boys who preferred religion from a distance hung around the grocery store or sat under a tree drinking soda pop. Nothing had changed.

Beverly Courtney
Crook
Twentieth century

IN those days there were one or two churches in London which still kept the custom of making specific charges for seats. There were free seats too, but if one arrived too late to fill one, one was charged sixpence or a shilling. I was not allowed to set out for Mass until after I had made the beds and done the washing-up at home. Sometimes, as on this particular day, this meant that I could only go to a church where there was a Mass at twelve o'clock. This in its turn meant a long walk. There was no local Mass at twelve o'clock.

On this day I set out, without a penny in my pocket, to walk to a twelve o'clock Mass in a fashionable district. It was a considerable distance from my home, and I arrived only just in time. Alas, all the free seats were taken. I looked round in confusion and saw that there was just one empty seat among the sixpennys, and slipped into that.

I had scarcely knelt down and hidden my face, which was scarlet, when the verger prodded me in the ribs with a collecting bag on the end of a long cane.

"I will go up to the altar of God," said the priest at the altar. "To God, the giver of youth and happiness."

"Sixpence," said the verger, and prodded me again.

I looked up and shook my head.

"Sixpence," said the verger, and went on prodding.

"I haven't got sixpence," I whispered.

"All right, then," said the verger, "you must go into the free seats."

"There isn't one," I said.

"Well, then, sixpence."

I was scalded. There was a priest standing in the aisle watching the scene. When I sprang to my feet and pushed out of the sixpenny seats, he came forward and put his hand on my shoulder.

"You are not going, child?" he said. I shook him off.

"Yes, I am, and I will never come to Mass again."

I went, beginning the long walk home again, hardly able to stop my tears of rage.

"Thou, O God, art all my strength, why hast thou cast me off?" said the priest at the altar. "Why do I go mourning, with enemies pressing me hard?"

Caryll Houselander
Twentieth century

COME you all: Enter into the joy of our Lord. You the first and you the last, receive alike your reward; you rich and you poor, dance together; you sober and you weaklings, celebrate the day; you who have kept the fast and you who have not, rejoice today. The table is richly loaded: Enjoy its royal banquet. The calf is a fatted one: Let no one go away hungry. All of you enjoy the banquet of faith; all of you receive the riches of his goodness.

Let none grieve over their poverty, for the universal kingdom has been revealed; let none weep over their sins, for pardon has shone from the grave; let none fear death, for the death of our Savior has set us free.

Saint John Chrysostom
Fourth century

ON the day of the resurrection of the Lord, which we call "the Lord's Day," you must always gather to give thanks to God and to bless him for all the benefits he has heaped upon us through Christ, by rescuing us from the bonds of ignorance and error.

Let your sacrifice be spotless and pleasing to God, who has said of his ecumenical Church:

> "In every place, they will present to me
> incense and a pure offering
> For I am a great king,
> says the Lord Almighty,
> and my name is wonderful among the nations"
> (Malachi 1:11, 14).

Apostolic Constitutions
Fourth century

Lord, shall we not bring these gifts to Your service?
Shall we not bring to Your service all our powers
For life, for dignity, grace and order,
And intellectual pleasures of the senses?
The LORD who created must wish us to create
And employ our creation again in His service
Which is already His service in creating.
For Man is joined spirit and body,
And therefore must serve as spirit and body.
Visible and invisible, two worlds meet in Man;
Visible and invisible must meet in His Temple;
You must not deny the body.

Now you shall see the Temple completed:
After much striving, after many obstacles;
For the work of creation is never without travail;
The formed stone, the visible crucifix,
The dressed altar, the lifting light,
    Light
    Light
The visible reminder of Invisible Light.

T. S. Eliot
Twentieth century

THE Day of the Sun is the day on which we all gather in a common meeting, because it is the first day, the day on which God, changing darkness and matter, created the world; and it is the day on which Jesus Christ our Savior rose from the dead. For He was crucified on the day before that of Kronos (26); and on the day after that of Kronos, which is the Day of the Sun, He appeared to His Apostles and disciples, and taught them these things which we have also submitted to you for your consideration.

Saint Justin Martyr
Second century

LL people that on earth do dwell,
   Sing to the Lord with cheerful voice;
Him serve with mirth, his praise forth tell,
   Come ye before him, and rejoice.

The Lord, ye know, is God indeed;
   Without our aid he did us make;
We are his folk, he doth us feed,
   And for his sheep he doth us take.

Oh enter then his gates with praise,
   Approach with joy his courts unto;
Praise, laud and bless his name always.
   For it is seemly so to do.

For why, the Lord our God is good;
   His mercy is for ever sure;
His truth at all times firmly stood,
   And shall from age to age endure.

William Kethe
Sixteenth century

T is important to devote attention to the *songs used by the assembly,* since singing is a particularly apt way to express a joyful heart, accentuating the solemnity of the celebration and fostering the sense of a common faith and a shared love.

Pope John Paul II
Twentieth century

AKE a joyful noise to the LORD, all the earth.
   Worship the LORD with gladness;
   come into his presence with singing.

Know that the LORD is God.
   It is he that made us, and we are his;
   we are his people, and the sheep of his pasture.

Enter his gates with thanksgiving,
   and his courts with praise.
   Give thanks to him, bless his name.

For the LORD is good;
> his steadfast love endures forever,
> and his faithfulness to all generations.

Psalm 100

IT is not surprising that music and song are so closely linked with the praise of divinity. As Saint Augustine observed long ago, whoever sings "prays twice," in music as well as words. From its very origin, the Christian community sang. In the New Testament, Paul's letters are punctuated by doxologies, hymn fragments, and references to the practice of singing in worshipping assemblies. . . .

The Christian church was born singing the songs of ancient Israel, the synagogue, and the Greco-Roman world. Psalms and canticles formed the heart of prayer and the music of the earliest Christian assemblies. Luke's Gospel barely gets through the second chapter without bursting into song four times: Mary sings that her soul magnifies the Lord, Zechariah sings blessing to the Lord of Israel, the angels near Bethlehem sing "Glory to God in the highest," and old Simeon sings his farewell song of peace. Each of these songs became regular parts of Christian daily prayer within the first two centuries. Saint Augustine, writing in the fourth century, could observe: "Apart from those moments when the scriptures are being read or a sermon is preached, when the bishop is praying aloud or the deacon is speaking the intention of the litany of community prayer, is there any time when the faithful assembled are not singing?"

Don E. Saliers
Twentieth century

IT is not you that sings, it is the Church that is singing, and you, as a member, . . . may share in its song. Thus all singing together that is right must serve to widen our spiritual horizon, make us see our little company as a member of the great Christian Church on earth, and help us willingly and gladly to join our singing, be it feeble or good, to the song of the Church.

Dietrich Bonhoeffer
Twentieth century

TAMBOURINES!
Tambourines!
Tambourines
To the glory of God!
Tambourines
To glory!

A gospel shout
And a gospel song:
Life is short
But God is long!

Tambourines!
Tambourines!
Tambourines
To glory!

Langston Hughes
Twentieth century

ALL you peoples, clap your hands;
    shout to God with joyful cries.
For the LORD, the Most High, inspires awe,
    the great king over all the earth,
Who made people subject to us,
    brought nations under our feet,
Who chose a land for our heritage,
    the glory of Jacob, the beloved.

God mounts the throne amid shouts of joy;
    the LORD, amid trumpet blasts.
Sing praise to God, sing praise;
    sing praise to our king, sing praise.

God is king over all the earth;
    sing hymns of praise.
God rules over the nations;
    God sits upon his holy throne.

The princes of the peoples assemble
  with the people of the God of Abraham.
For the rulers of the earth belong to God,
  who is enthroned on high.

Psalm 47

DISTANT and soft on her ear fell the chimes from the
belfry of Christ Church,
While, intermingled with these, across the meadow were
wafted
Sounds of psalms, that were sung by the Swedes in their
church at Wicaco.

Henry Wadsworth
Longfellow
Nineteenth century

THEY began playing something Cass did not recognize,
something very slow, and more like the blues than a
hymn. Then it began to be more tense and more bitter and
more swift. The people in the chapel hummed low in their
throats and tapped their feet. Then the girl stepped forward.
She threw back her head and closed her eyes and that voice
rang out again:

Oh, that great getting-up morning,
Fare thee well, fare thee well!

Reverend Foster, standing on a height behind her, raised
both hands and mingled his voice with hers:

We'll be coming from every nation,
Fare thee well, fare thee well!

The chapel joined them . . .

James Baldwin
Twentieth century

T HEN the singing enveloped me. It was furry and reso-
nant, coming from everyone's very heart. There was no
sense of performance or judgment, only that the music was
breath and food.

Something inside me that was stiff and rotting would feel
soft and tender. Somehow the singing wore down all the
boundaries and distinctions that kept me so isolated. Sitting
there, standing with them to sing, sometimes so shaky and
sick that I felt like I might tip over, I felt bigger than myself,
like I was being taken care of, tricked into coming back   Anne Lamott
to life.   Twentieth century

O come, all you people!
Let us sing the praises
of the Savior's third-day Resurrection,
for we have been delivered by it
from the unbreakable bonds of hell,
and, having received incorruption and life,
let us cry out:
O crucified, buried and risen Lord,
save us by Your Resurrection,
for You only love Your whole creation!   Byzantine liturgy

L ET us praise our Maker, with true passion extol Him.
Let the whole creation give out another sweetness,
Nicer in our nostrils, a novel fragrance
From cleansed occasions in accord together
As one feeling fabric, all flushed and intact,
Phenomena and numbers announcing in one
Multitudinous œcumenical song
Their grand givenness of gratitude and joy,
Peaceable and plural, their positive truth
An authoritative This, an unthreatened Now

When, in love and in laughter, each lives itself,
For, united by His Word, cognition and power,
System and Order, are a single glory,
And the pattern is complex, their places safe.

W. H. Auden
Twentieth century

I myself shall now set down the practices of the Christian community. . . . We come together in an assembly and congregation to surround God with prayer, as if in battle formation. . . . We gather together to consider the divine Scriptures. . . . And at the same time there is encouragement, correction and holy censure.

Tertullian
Third century

I N the middle the reader is to stand upon something high and read the books of Moses, of Joshua the son of Nun, of Judges and Kings, of Chronicles and those from after the return, and in readings let someone else sing the hymns of David, and let the people respond with verses. After this let our Acts be read and the epistles of Paul our fellow worker, which he sent to the churches under the guidance of the Holy Spirit; and after these let a deacon or priest read the Gospels, which I, Matthew, and John have transmitted to you, and which the co-workers of Paul, Luke and Mark, have received and passed on to you.

Apostolic Constitutions
Fourth century

I N considering the Sunday eucharist more than thirty years after the Council, we need to assess how well the word of God is being proclaimed and how effectively the People of God have grown in knowledge and love of sacred scripture. There are two aspects of this—that of *celebration* and that of *personal appropriation*—and they are very closely related. At the level of celebration, the fact that the Council made it possible to proclaim the word of God in the language of the community taking part in the celebration must awaken a new sense of responsibility toward the word, allowing "the distinctive character of the sacred text" to shine forth "even in the mode of reading or singing." At the level of personal appropriation, the hearing of the word of God proclaimed must be well prepared in the souls of the faithful by an apt knowledge of scripture and, where pastorally possible, by *special initiatives designed to deepen understanding of the biblical readings,* particularly those used on Sundays and holy days. If Christian individuals and families are not regularly drawing new life from the reading of the sacred text in a spirit of prayer and docility to the church's interpretation, then it is difficult for the liturgical proclamation of the word of God alone to produce the fruit we might expect. This is the value of initiatives in parish communities that bring together during the week those who take part in the eucharist—priest, ministers and faithful—in order to prepare the Sunday liturgy, reflecting beforehand upon the word of God that will be proclaimed. The objective sought here is that the entire celebration—praying, singing, listening, and not just the preaching—should express in some way the theme of Sunday liturgy, so that all those taking part may be penetrated more powerfully by it. Clearly, much depends on those who exercise the ministry of the word. It is their duty to prepare the reflection on the word of the Lord by prayer and study of the sacred text, so that they may then express its contents faithfully and apply them to people's concerns and to their daily lives.

It should also be borne in mind that the *liturgical proclamation of the word of God,* especially in the eucharistic assembly, is not so much a time for meditation and catechesis as a *dialogue between God and his people,* a dialogue in which the wonders of salvation are proclaimed and the demands of the covenant are continually restated. On their part, the People of God are drawn to respond to this dialogue of love by giving thanks and praise, also by demonstrating their fidelity to the task of continual conversion.

Pope John Paul II
Twentieth century

THE gospel writers . . . were highly developed spiritually, and they crafted stories, in the memory and style of Jesus, that were meant to communicate spiritual truth. Our effort is to attune ourselves to their art so that we may receive their gift. When the incognito risen Christ walked with the two disciples on the road to Emmaus, he opened the scriptures for them. The result was their hearts burned and their eyes saw. Is not this the ultimate reason we read sacred writings?

John Shea
Twentieth century

MUCH Gesture, from the Pulpit—
Strong Hallelujahs roll—
Narcotics cannot still the Tooth
That nibbles at the soul—

Emily Dickinson
Nineteenth century

ALL Scripture is inspired by God for our benefit; it was composed by the Spirit for this reason. . . . "Care," it is said, "makes the greatest sin to cease." Now the Prophets teach certain things, the Historians and the Law teach others, and Proverbs provides still a different sort of advice, but the Book of Psalms encompasses the benefit of them all. It foretells what is to come and memorializes history; it legislates for life, gives advice on practical matters, and serves in general as a repository of good teachings, carefully searching out what is suitable for each individual.

Saint Basil
Fourth century

Come, let us gather round the table.
Light the candles. Steward, pour the wine.
It is dark outside. The streets are noisy
with the scurrying of rats, with shoddy
tarts, shills, thugs, harsh shouting.

And what comfort is cold within? We're able
to offer a slim repast. The taste of brine,
warm from fresh tears, is in the glass. Choosy
guests will not come here. The bread is body
broken. The wine is dark with blood. I'm doubting

if half of those invited will turn up.
Most will prefer a different table,
will go elsewhere with gentler foods to sup.
And yet this is indeed a wedding feast
and we rejoice to share the bitter cup,
the crumbs of bread. For O my Lord, not least
of all that makes us raise the glass, is that we toast
You, who assembled this uncomely group: our one
mysterious host.

Madeleine L'Engle
Twentieth century

You probably need to eat something," the baker said. "I hope you'll eat some of my hot rolls. You have to eat and keep going. Eating is a small, good thing in a time like this," he said.

He served them warm cinnamon rolls just out of the oven, the icing still runny. He put butter on the table and knives to spread the butter. Then the baker sat down at the table with them. He waited. He waited until they each took a roll from the platter and began to eat. "It's good to eat something," he said, watching them. "There's more. Eat up. Eat all you want. There's all the rolls in the world in here."

They ate rolls and drank coffee. Ann was suddenly hungry, and the rolls were warm and sweet. She ate three of them, which pleased the baker. Then he began to talk. They listened carefully. Although they were tired and in anguish, they listened to what the baker had to say. They nodded when the baker began to speak of loneliness, and of the sense of doubt and limitation that had come to him in his middle years. He told them what it was like to be childless all these years. To repeat the days with the ovens endlessly full and endlessly empty. The party food, the celebrations he'd worked over. Icing knuckle-deep. The tiny wedding couples stuck into cakes. Hundreds of them, no, thousands by now. Birthdays. Just imagine all those candles burning. He had a necessary trade. He was a baker. He was glad he wasn't a florist. It was better to be feeding people. This was a better smell anytime than flowers.

"Smell this," the baker said, breaking open a dark loaf. "It's a heavy bread, but rich." They smelled it, then he had them taste it. It had the taste of molasses and coarse grains. They listened to him. They ate what they could. They swallowed the dark bread. It was like daylight under the fluorescent trays of light. They talked on into the early morning, the high, pale cast of light in the windows, and they did not think of leaving.

Raymond Carver
Twentieth century

O N the Lord's Day of the Lord gather together, break bread and give thanks, after confessing your transgressions so that your sacrifice may be pure. Let no one who has a quarrel with his neighbor join you until he is reconciled, lest your sacrifice be defiled. For this is that which was proclaimed by the Lord: "In every place and time let there be offered to Me a clean sacrifice. For I am a Great King," says the Lord, "and My name is wonderful among the gentiles."

Didache
First century

A lamb only becomes food because it is killed. Its "vocation" is to exist for the life of others; in a sense its fulfillment is to be slaughtered and eaten. The lamb for Passover was to be very carefully chosen, certified free of blemish, because its eating was an act dedicating the people to God. There is a certain ruthlessness in it. The focus of the message is that it is in his death that Jesus becomes the bread of life for others, and that it is in total engagement with his death that others are to find the ultimate satisfaction of their hunger, so that they will not hunger or thirst again.

Monika Hellwig
Twentieth century

THE paschal mystery of Jesus Christ is the central mystery celebrated by the church. The celebration is both expressive and formative of the community. Each day, each week, each season of the church year, the paschal mystery remains as the foundational memory from which the ongoing Christian story is created. New stories will be expressive of the transforming power. But always the same context will frame the meaning of the story. "Lord, by your cross and resurrection, you have set us free. You are the Savior of the world" (Eucharistic Acclamation D).

All Christian spirituality is formed from this mystery and leads to the mystery. The mystery, Christ manifest through his Body, the church, makes Christian spirituality an essentially communal spirituality. From the beginning of his teaching Jesus made the community nature of his mission clear. Discipleship was a public reality as well as a personal response. The twelve, symbols of the new Israel, are gathered from many different backgrounds. They and all disciples shall be sent to gather the lost, the sick, and the poor as a sign of the presence of the new age of God's reign. The community is called to be salt for the earth and light for the world. As a leaven is used to form new dough, so the community shall be used to point to the way all people are meant to live in the covenant mystery of God. The power of the resurrection reaches the world through this new creation. The community is the Body that is given for all. . . .

The liturgical life of the church provides a daily, weekly, and seasonal environment for spiritual direction of the Christian community. Ritualized moments of the Christian life focus the meaning of personal journeying within the pilgrim community. Thus the liturgical life of the church, accenting seasonal rhythms of the paschal mystery, provides an environment that embraces the dying and rising in every life.

Shawn Madigan
Twentieth century

THE eucharist is already a meal, and the Bible's favourite picture for the final kingdom is that of feasting. At the eucharist Christ is present to the eyes of faith: at His table in the final kingdom we shall see Him face to face (cf. 1 Corinthians 13:12a). The eucharist is a periodic celebration: in the final kingdom the worship and rejoicing, as in the life of heaven, will be perpetual. In the eucharist a part of . . . the world serve the glory of God: in the final kingdom God will be all in all. The people who celebrate the eucharist are imperfect in their obedience: in the final kingdom their submission to the rule of God will be total. Eucharistic joy is marred by our persistence in sin: the joy of the final kingdom will be full.

Geoffrey Wainwright
Twentieth century

I saw the throng, so deeply separate,
    Fed at one only board—
The devout people, moved, intent, elate,
    And the devoted Lord.

Oh struck apart! not side from human side,
    But soul from human soul
As each asunder absorbed the multiplied,
    The ever unparted whole.

I saw this people as a field of flowers,
    Each grown at such a price
The sum of unimaginable powers
    Did no more than suffice.

A thousand single central daisies they,
    A thousand of the one;
For each, the entire monopoly of day;
    For each, the whole of the devoted sun.

Alice Meynell
Nineteenth century

At this table we put aside every worldly separation based on culture, class, or other differences. Baptized, we no longer admit to distinctions based on age or sex or race or wealth. This communion is why all prejudice, all racism, all sexism, all deference to wealth and power must be banished from our parishes, our homes, and our lives. This communion is why we will not call enemies those who are human beings like ourselves. This communion is why we will not commit the world's resources to an escalating arms race while the poor die. We cannot. Not when we have feasted here on the "body broken" and "blood poured out" for the life of the world.

Let that be clear in the reverent way we walk forward to take the holy bread and cup. Let it be clear in the way ministers of communion announce: "The body of Christ," "The blood of Christ." Let it be clear in our "Amen!" Let it be clear in the songs and psalms we sing and the way we sing them. Let it be clear in the holy silence that fills this church when all have partaken.

Before coming forward we say, "Lord, I am not worthy." We are never worthy of this table, for it is God's grace and gift. Yet we do come forward. This is "food for the journey" that we began at baptism. We may eat of it when we are tired, when we are discouraged, even when we have failed. But not when we have forgotten the church, forgotten the way we began at the font; not when we have abandoned our struggle against evil and remain unrepentant for having done so. Let us examine our lives honestly each time before approaching the eucharist. "Worthy" none of us ever is, but properly prepared each one of us must be. Christ, present in the eucharist and in us, calls us to be a holy communion, to grow in love and holiness for one another's sake.

Joseph Cardinal
Bernardin
Twentieth century

THE day of the resurrection, which sheds its light upon the entire year and transfigures it, also penetrates the smallest units of our time. That is what we, together with Jesus, ask of his Father and ours: "Give us this day our necessary bread," the bread of "this day." The sacramental day that transforms each moment of our lives into new time is *Sunday*, the "Lord's Day" (Revelation 1:10). Because of the Eucharist, Sunday is indeed the efficacious memorial, the fruitful anamnesis that makes us present to the eternal liturgy and participants in it. It is the day of the assembly in which we really receive a foretaste of the communion of all the saints in the Blessed Trinity. It is the day on which through us our world mysteriously enters into the freedom of the children of God for which it groans and which it anxiously awaits. Far from being a "holiday," it is the day on which "the Father still goes on working" (John 5:17) and grants us to share intensely in his creative and saving love. It is a day of rest indeed, but of the Rest of God in which the energy expended does not lead to the exhaustion of death but is an outpouring of life, joy, festivity, and creative liturgy.

Through the *prayer of the Hours* the mystery of the liturgy that is celebrated on Sunday permeates and transfigures the time of daily life. . . . The office is our incarnate participation in the prayer of Jesus himself. The prayer which the Word makes to the Father expands and, in the form of praise, takes flesh in us who are in synergy with the Holy Spirit. The office is a prism allowing the pure light of the Son's own praise to be channeled through the adopted children of God.

Jean Corbon
Twentieth century

ABBA Poemen said, "It is written: 'As the hart longs for flowing streams, so longs my soul for Thee, O God.' (Psalm 42:1) For truly harts in the desert devour many reptiles and when their venom burns them, they try to come to the springs, to drink so as to assuage the venom's burning. It is the same for the monks: sitting in the desert they are burned by the venom of evil demons, and they long for Saturday and Sunday to come to be able to go to the springs of water, that is to say, the body and blood of the Lord, so as to be purified from the bitterness of the evil one."

Sayings of the
Desert Fathers

And now the time has come for us to *return into the world.* "Let us depart in peace," says the celebrant as he leaves the altar, and this is the last *commandment* of the liturgy. We must not stay on Mount Tabor, although we know that it is good for us to be there. We are sent back. But now "we have seen the true Light, we have received the heavenly Spirit." And it is as witnesses of this Light, as witnesses of the Spirit, that we must "go forth" and begin the never-ending mission of the Church. Eucharist was the *end* of the journey, the end of time. And now it is again the *beginning,* and things that were impossible are again revealed to us as possible. The time of the world has become the time of the Church, the time of salvation and redemption. And God has made us *competent,* as Paul Claudel has said, competent to be His witnesses, to fulfill what He has done and is ever doing. This is the meaning of the Eucharist; this is why the mission of the Church begins in the liturgy of ascension, for it alone makes possible the liturgy of mission.

Alexander
Schmemann
Twentieth century

Once the assembly disperses, Christ's disciples return to their everyday surroundings with the commitment to make their whole life a gift, a spiritual sacrifice pleasing to God (cf. Romans 12:1). They feel indebted to their brothers and sisters because of what they have received in the celebration, not unlike the disciples of Emmaus who, once they had recognized the Risen Christ "in the breaking of the bread" (cf. Luke 24:30–32), felt the need to return immediately to share with their brothers and sisters the joy of meeting the Lord (cf. Luke 24:33–35).

Pope John Paul II
Twentieth century

At Our Lady of the Angels this Sunday the announcements are a transition from the final quiet and peace of the Communion to the sending forth. The various activities of the week are announced, then all stand and the presider prays the blessing and the dismissal. A concluding song leads to much visiting and to the procession out. I mean the true procession of this Church: one, two, and five at a time going back to neighborhoods and homes, roles and jobs, studies and waiting. But Sunday by Sunday the world is here being transformed in Christ!

Cardinal Roger
Mahony
Twentieth century

THE first day of creation
Is dawning in the soul,
Upon the deep God hovers
Where fear and chaos roll.
The inward dark is parting,
The seas make room for land.
Great shorelines are emerging,
A new world is at hand!

Yet God is recreating
More than our inner world:
Look up beyond the planets
Where galaxies are swirled.
Look out and see how often
Surprising love is shown.
Christ is at work reshaping
Both stars and hearts of stone.

All life in Christ is compassed
By that transforming grace
Which spins new worlds and wonders
In ev'ry time and place.
O Twirler of the stardust,
O Light no darkness rims,
Your new creation pulses
With worship, praise, and hymns.

Thomas H. Troeger
Twentieth century

O quanta qualia sunt illa sabbata
Quae semper celebrat superna curia!
Quae fessis requies, quae merces fortibus,
Cum erit omnia Deus in omnibus!

Vere Jerusalem est illa civitas,
Cujus pax jugis est, summa jucunditas,
Ubi non praevenit rem desiderium,
Nec desiderio minus est praemium.

O how great and how wonderful is the Sabbath which the court of heaven celebrates for ever! What rest for the weary, what reward for the valiant, when God will be all in all!

That city is well called Jerusalem, whose peace is everlasting, whose joy is supreme. There desire never overtakes fulfillment and the reward never falls short of the desire.

Abelard
Twelfth century

S UNDAY is the *first* day, the day when the Creator began creating, separating the light from the darkness. Sunday is the day of beginning, the day of light-separated-from-darkness, the day when God first looked at creation and called it good.

What better day to see Christ rise? So the first day is also the *third* day, the day on which Christ rose from the dead. And on the third day, Magdalene and her two companions— a trinity of women—came to know God as savior and redeemer. For when they went to the cemetery in the darkness before dawn, they were dazzled by the glory of a handsome angel and a neatly folded shroud in an otherwise empty tomb. That morning is brighter than all others since the beginning. And when the sun set that Sunday, while the apostles were huddled together shaking their heads in disbelief at what Magdalene had told them, the risen Lord appeared in their midst (like a match struck in the dark) and said "Peace be with you.". . . Sunday is the day of the life-born-out-of-death.

Sunday is the day that the Holy Spirit came. According to the Gospel of John, it was on that first Easter evening that Jesus gave the Spirit. According to the Acts of the Apostles, it was 50 days after Easter—but still a Sunday—when wind shook the house and fire burned understanding into the brains of the apostles. They spilled into the streets of Jerusalem and preached so ferociously and with such joy that people thought they were drunk! Sunday is the day when the church began its mission. The first day is the *fiftieth* day—the day after seven weeks of seven days when all things come around full circle. The day of creation is the day of re-creation; the day when Christ rose is the day that the Spirit descended. . . .

For our ancestors, the name "Day of the Lord" had deep meaning. The "Day of the Lord" was the biblical name given by the prophets to the last day, the end of time when the Living God would appear on earth to work justice for the poor. The early church came to interpret the last day as the day Christ would return in glory and judge the living and the dead. So for the church, the first day, which is also the third day, which is also the fiftieth day, is most importantly the *eighth* day. Because there are only seven days in the week as we know it, the *eighth* day is a sign of eternity's dawn, the time beyond time, a rehearsal for the day that will last forever. Sunday is the day of heaven-on-earth and earth-becoming-heaven.

David Philippart
Twentieth century

Oo Oo Come Sunday,
oh, come Sunday, that's the day.
Lord, dear Lord above, God Almighty, God of love,
please look down and see my people through.

I believe that God put sun and moon up in the sky.
I don't mind the gray skies,
cause they're just clouds passing by.

Heaven is a goodness time, a brighter light on high.
Do unto others as you would have them do unto you,
and have a brighter by and by.

I believe God is now, was then, and always will be.
With God's blessing
we can make it through eternity.

Duke Ellington
Twentieth century

LIFE without end? It is here that Christians notice a paradox. The Lord's Day is the day of eternity—a span of time meant to anticipate timelessness. Time as a sign of timelessness, what a delightful contradiction! That is why Christians can call the Lord's Day "the eighth day of the week." What "eighth day" means is a day that transcends the other seven. It's as if the Lord's Day leaps out of the week altogether, as if the blessed Sabbath—the seventh day— doesn't come to an end, but lasts forever.

Peter Mazar
Twentieth century

THIS is the day when light was first created,
Symbol and gift of order and design.
In light is God's intention clearly stated,
The break of day reveals this loving mind.

This is the day of our complete surprising,
Repeat of Easter: Christ has come to life!
Now is the feast of love's revolt and rising
Against the rule of hell and death and grief.

We join to praise, with ev'ry race and nation,
The God who with the world his Spirit shares;
Strong wind of change and earth's illumination,
Dispelling static thoughts and darkest fears.

This is the day of worship and of vision,
Great birthday of the church in ev'ry land.
Let Christians all confess their sad division,
And seek the strength again as one to stand.

We pray that this, the day of recreation,
May hallow all the week that is to come.
Help us, O Lord, to lay a good foundation
For all we do at work, at school, at home.

Fred Kaan
Twentieth century

THUS we all look to the East when we pray but few of us know that we are seeking our old country, Paradise, which *God planted in Eden in the East* (Genesis 2:8). We pray standing, on the first day of the week, but we do not all know the reason. On the day of resurrection, rising up we remind ourselves of the grace given to us by standing at prayer, not only because we rose with Christ and are bound to *seek those things which are above* (Colossians 3:1), but because the day seems to us to be somehow an image of the age which we await wherefore, though it is "the beginning of days" it is not called by Moses "first," but "one." For he says, *there was evening and there was morning, one day* (Genesis 1:5), as though the same day often recurred. Now "one" and "eight" are the same, in itself distinctly indicating that really "one" and "eight" of which the Psalmist makes mention in certain titles of the psalms, the state which follows after this present time, the day which knows no waning or eventide, and no successor, that age which ends not or grows old. Of necessity, then, the Church teaches her foster-children to offer their prayers on that day standing so that through a continual reminder of the endless life we may not neglect to make provision for our passing on to that place.

Saint Basil
Fourth century

SOME judge one day to be better than another, while others judge all days to be alike. Let all be fully convinced in their own minds. Those who observe the day, observe it in honor of the Lord. Also those who eat, eat in honor of the Lord, since they give thanks to God; while those who abstain, abstain in honor of the Lord and give thanks to God.

We do not live to ourselves, and we do not die to ourselves. If we live, we live to the Lord, and if we die, we die to the Lord; so then, whether we live or whether we die, we are the Lord's. For to this end Christ died and lived again, so that he might be Lord of both the dead and the living.

Romans 14:5–9

HE also ordained that one day should be set aside as a special day for prayer: I mean that which is truly the first and chief of all, the day of our Lord and Savior. . . . The same observance was recommended by this blessed prince to all classes of his subjects: his earnest desire being gradually to lead all mankind to the worship of God. Accordingly he enjoined on all the subjects of the Roman empire to observe the Lord's Day, as a day of rest, and also to honor the day which precedes the Sabbath, in memory, I suppose, of what the Savior of mankind is recorded to have achieved on that day. And since his desire was to teach his whole army zealously to honor the Savior's day (which derives its name from light, and from the sun), he freely granted to those among them who were partakers of the divine faith, leisure for attendance on the services of the Church of God, in order that they might be able to perform their religious worship. [Concerning the emperor Constantine.]

Eusebius
Third–Fourth century

CHRIST, having trampled upon death this day,
according to His word,
rose up bestowing joy on the whole world,
that all of us, shouting this hymn, might say:
O Font of life, of Light unapproachable by humanity,
O almighty Savior, have mercy on us!

Byzantine liturgy

AS the German lines crumbled in the final stages of the Second World War, Deitrich Bonhoeffer was loaded into a woodburning van with fifteen other Buchenwald inmates. With their arms pinned to their sides, and with nothing to eat or drink, they began their hellish journey in quest of other prison accommodations. When the van broke down, they spent a cold and stormy night in the bomb craters. An entire day was lost in trying to get the prisoners across the Danube. Finding at last a pontoon that had not been bombed, they crossed the river and spent the night in the Bavarian village of Schoonberg. The next day was Sunday, and Payne Best recounts how Bonhoeffer held a little service of divine worship, speaking words which reached the hearts of all, and expressing the spirit of their imprisonment and the resolves it had brought. Hardly had he concluded his last prayer when two evil-looking men opened the door and ordered him to prepare to leave with them, a command which had come to mean one thing only—the scaffold.

And so, as his fellow prisoners bade him good-bye, Bonhoeffer completed the last Sunday celebration of his life. Though the circumstances in which he and his fellow prisoners observed Sunday were unusual, what they did was not. Christians have always gathered on the Lord's Day mutually to admonish and comfort one another with God's Word and to engage in prayer.

In fact, were a man from Mars to observe us from his space platform, the most obvious evidence he would have that there are Christians on this planet would be their gathering on the first day of each week at some appointed place and time. . . . Though great differences would appear in these gatherings—some would be kneeling before an altar shrouded in the smoke of incense, some wailing Psalms as given out by a presenter, some shouting and lifting up their hands in an ecstasy of religious enthusiasm, some sitting quietly absorbing in sober meditation—yet all would be doing so on the self-same day. White Christians and black Christians would gather on the same day; Orthodox, Roman Catholic and Protestant Christians, Christians in Commmunist as well as in non-Communist countries—all would meet on the first day of the week.

Paul K. Jewett
Twentieth century

ONLY on the first day of the week did the church choose to invent a name different than the Jewish name. The Jews call the day after the sabbath the "first day" of the week. Christians call it "The Lord's Day."

The "Day of the Lord" is a title straight from the mouths of the Jewish prophets. It meant something like Doom's Day or Judgment Day (not exactly a day to plan a Sunday picnic).

"The Lord's Day" is a title also found in Christian scriptures, especially among Christians expecting Doom's Day any minute. . . . In this sense, "Lord's Day" meant the day of the great epiphany, the coming of God to right all wrongs and to establish the reign of glory in heaven and peace on earth.

The Christian Lord's Day took on other meanings from the first day of the week. That's the day creation began, when God said, "Let there be light." The Lord's Day is a day of beginnings, a day of light separated from darkness.

Peter Mazar
Twentieth century

SPIRIT of mercy, truth and love,
O shed thine influence from above,
and still from age to age convey
the wonders of this sacred day.

In every clime, by every tongue,
be God's amazing glory sung;
may all the listening earth be taught
the acts our great Redeemer wrought.

Unfailing comfort, heavenly guide,
still o'er thy holy church preside;
still let mankind thy blessings prove,
Spirit of mercy, truth and love.

Anonymous
Eighteenth century

THE bishop should therefore ensure that in his diocese the idea of the Lord's day as the first holy day of all is proposed to the devotion of the faithful and taught to them in such a way that it may become in fact a day of joy and freedom from work.

Ceremonial of Bishops

Now what exactly do we mean by the phrase: the day of the Lord? It could mean: the day which belongs to God, the day on which we must fulfil our duty of adoring God. Beyond doubt the adoration of God, divine service, is the very first of Sunday's duties. It is of immense importance that this day, as old as Christianity itself, should stand out and direct our minds above, just as the church steeple stands out above all the houses of the villages and points up to heaven. But why must this day be Sunday rather than any other day of the week? Why was not the Sabbath of the Old Testament retained for this purpose?

The answer lies precisely in the name itself—the Lord's day. For this means the day on which *Christ the Lord,* after suffering death for our sakes on the Cross, proved himself to be *the Lord,* the one who had the power to lead us, too, out of the abyss of death into the glory of resurrection.

The Lord's day therefore means *"Christ's day.". . .*

The title "the day of the Lord" is to be found in use in apostolic times. For St. John the Apostle relates at the beginning of his Apocalypse (1:10) that it was "on the Lord's day" that he was taken by the Spirit and heard heavenly voices. And from that time onwards, throughout every century, Sunday has been referred to as the Lord's day: in Greek it was know as *Kyriake* (from *Kyrios,* the Lord); in Latin as *dominica* (from *dominus,* the Lord). All the romance languages use words derived from this root: the French *dimanche,* the Italian *domenica,* the Spanish *domingo.* Only in Teutonic languages has the pre-Christian name of Sunday been retained.

Josef A. Jungmann
Twentieth century

The Day of the Lord, or the Day of the Resurrection, is indeed the true day of every Christian: for this reason it is called the Lord's Day, because on that day the Lord ascended triumphant to the Father. And if this day is called Sunday by the pagans, we too are most ready to confess that today the Light of the World has risen, that today the Sun of Justice has risen.

Jerome
Fourth century

THE martyrs of Abitina (near Medjez el Bab in Tunisia), . . . might well be called "martyrs for Sunday." Thirty-one men and eighteen women arrested for illegal assembly appeared before Proconsul Anulinus in Carthage on February 12, 304. When the official accused them of disobeying the imperial edicts, Saturninus, a priest, answered: "We must celebrate the Lord's Day. It is a law for us." Emeritus, a lector, in whose home the community had assembled, spoke to the same effect: "Yes, it was in my house that we celebrated the Lord's Day. We cannot live without celebrating the Lord's Day." And Victoria, a virgin, proudly declared: "I attended the meeting because I am a Christian."

P. Jounel
Twentieth century

SUNDAY, on which by apostolic tradition the paschal mystery is celebrated, must be observed in the universal Church as the primordial holy day of obligation.

On Sundays and other holy days of obligation, the faithful are obliged to participate in the Mass. Moreover, they are to abstain from those works and affairs which hinder the worship to be rendered to God, the joy proper to the Lord's day, or the suitable relaxation of mind and body.

Canon Law 1246
and 1247

THIS *is the day which the Lord hath made,*
    Shining like Eden absolved of sin,
Three parts glitter to one part shade:
    Let us be glad and rejoice therein.

Everything's scoured brighter than metal.
    Everything sparkles as pure glass—
The leaf on the poplar, the zinnia's petal,
    The wing of the bird, and the blade of the grass.

All, all is luster. The glossy harbor
    Dazzles the gulls that, gleaming, fly.

Glimmers the wasp on the grape in the arbor.
  Glisten the clouds in the polished sky.

Tonight—tomorrow—the leaf will fade,
  The waters tarnish, the dark begin.
But *this is the day which the Lord hath made:*
  Let us be glad and rejoice therein.

Phyllis McGinley
Twentieth century

O God, you make us glad with the weekly remembrance of the glorious resurrection of your Son our Lord: Give us this day such blessings through our worship of you, that the week to come may be spent in your favor; through Jesus Christ our Lord.

The Book of
Common Prayer

COME, let us with our Lord arise,
Our Lord Who made both earth and skies;
Who died to save the world He made
And rose triumphant from the dead;
He rose, the Prince of life and peace,
And stamped the day forever His.

This is the day the Lord hath made
That all may see His love displayed,
May feel His resurrection's power
And rise again to fall no more,
In perfect righteousness renewed,
And filled with all the life of God.

Then let us render Him His own,
With solemn prayer approach the throne;
With meekness hear the gospel word,
With thanks His dying love record;
Our joyful hearts and voices raise
And fill His courts with songs of praise.

Charles Wesley
Eighteenth century

CHRIST crucified sets me on high;
Christ put to death raises me with Himself;
Christ grants me life;
therefore clapping my hands with joy
I sing unto the Savior a song of victory,
for He has been glorified.

Byzantine liturgy

WE celebrate Sunday because of the venerable resurrection of our Lord Jesus Christ, and we do so not
only at Easter but also at each turning of the week.

Pope Innocent I
Fifth century

OUT in the rain a world is growing green,
    On half the trees quick buds are seen
        Where glued-up buds have been.
Out in the rain God's Acre stretches green,
    Its harvest quick tho' still unseen:
        For there the Life hath been.

If Christ hath died His brethren well may die,
    Sing in the gate of death, lay by
        This life without a sigh:
For Christ hath died and good it is to die;
    To sleep when so He lays us by,
        Then wake without a sigh.

Yea, Christ hath died, yea, Christ is risen again:
    Wherefore both life and death grow plain
        To us who wax and wane;
For Christ Who rose shall die no more again:
    Amen: till He makes all things plain
        Let us wax on and wane.

Christina Rossetti
Nineteenth century

AND on the day of our Lord's resurrection, which is the Lord's Day, meet more diligently, sending praise to God that made the universe by Jesus, and sent Him to us, and allowed Him to suffer, and raised Him from the dead. Otherwise what apology will he make to God who does not assemble on that day to hear the saving word concerning the resurrection, on which we pray three times, standing in memory of Him who arose in three days, in which is performed the reading of the prophets, the preaching of the Gospel and the oblation of the sacrifice, the gift of the holy food?

Apostolic Constitutions
Fourth century

PRAISE . . . to the living one and giver of life, who tasted death of his own will; to the deathless one, who died in the flesh and gave life to mortal men; who was laid in the grave and raised up those who were in the grave; who slept among the dead and awakened those who were sleeping; who rose from the grave and raised up those who were fallen; who was raised up in glory and gave joy to his disciples; who was taken up on high and made those below to ascend; who fulfilled his promise and perfected those who were in need; to whom belongs glory . . . .

Antiochian Syrian
liturgy

Saint Jerome
Fourth century

SUNDAY is the day of the resurrection, it is the day of Christians, it is our day.

INTO creation's lowest parts descending,
And bursting by Thy might th' infernal chain
That bound the pris'ners, Thou at three days' ending,
As Jonah from the deep, hast ris'n again.

Thou didst not break the seal, Thy surety's token,
Arising from the tomb, Who left in birth

The portals of virginity unbroken
Opening the gate of heaven to sons of earth.

Thou, Sacrifice ineffable and living,
Didst to the Father by Thyself atone
As God eternal: resurrection giving
To Adam our first parent, by Thine own.

Saint John of
Damascus
Eighth century

What hard travail God does in death!
He strives in sleep, in our despair,
And all flesh shudders underneath
The nightmare of His sepulcher;

The earth shakes, grinding its deep stone;
All night the cold wind heaves and pries;
Creation strains sinew and bone
Against the dark door where He lies.

The stem bent, pent in seed, grows straight
And stands. Pain breaks in song. Surprising
The merely dead, graves fill with light
Like opened eyes. He rests in rising.

Wendell Berry
Twentieth century

Today Christ is risen from the tomb,
giving all the faithful eternal life—
and He gives back joy to the women bearing myrrh—
after the Passion, the Resurrection!

Byzantine liturgy

Gerard Manley
Hopkins
Nineteenth century

Let him easter in us, be a dayspring to the dimness of us,
be a crimson-cresseted east.

T HE prophets remind us that there is an *intrinsic* relationship between cult and conduct—that worship is an expression of, and not a substitute for, social responsibility. . . .

Justice cares for the establishment of right relationships. Justice implies the recognition within us and among us of our growth as unique human persons with gifts and grace, with potential and desires, with anxieties and hopes and fears. Justice includes unity and solidarity, the linking up of our destinies as brothers and sisters who rise and fall together without domination or constraint, without exploitation or manipulation, without discrimination or violence. . . .

While justice cares for the establishment of relationships, *liturgy* is their celebration. We gather to give praise and thanksgiving, to recall the mighty acts of God in human history, to make the memorial of Jesus' victorious death, to pray for the needs of our world, and to celebrate the kingdom of justice and love which is already and which is yet to be. Liturgy is our activity, our service as human persons in all our fragility and weakness, our hunger and thirst for justice still unsated, yet struggling to give expression to the life we are shaping in Christ. Liturgy is not a stepping outside of daily life into some mystical realm but a lifting up of our dailiness, recognizing that we are God-touched yet incomplete. It is a gathering of persons who need to let go, to give ourselves over, to surrender to the God of mystery, and to receive grace and strength to live no longer for ourselves. And in the very process of confessing the one true God and Jesus Christ whom God has sent, the confessing community's self-awareness is purified and deepened, its commitment to justice reaffirmed.

Kathleen Hughes
Twentieth century

C HRIST is indeed the Sun of Justice; and if to Him is joined the moon, that is His Church, full with His light, then in truth will He celebrate a new moon.

Origen
Third century

Now concerning the collection for the saints: you should follow the directions I gave to the churches of Galatia. On the first day of every week, each of you is to put aside and save whatever extra you earn.

    1 Corinthians 16:1–2

The word *congregation* does not mean "a gathering of many people"—not even of many pious and reverent people. Even in such a group that unifying, simultaneously fortifying and fervent quality which is the essence of the true congregation might be lacking. Christ defines it: "For where two or three are gathered together for my sake, there am I in the midst of them." The Acts of the Apostles gives more details in its report on the days following Pentecost: "And continuing daily with one accord in the temple, and breaking bread in their houses, they took their food with gladness and simplicity of heart, praising God and being in favor with all the people."

A congregation, then, exists when a number of people disciplined by faith and conscious of their membership in Christ gather to celebrate the sacred mysteries. Even then it does not follow effortlessly. . . .

If there is to be a congregation, the believers must know what a congregation is; they must desire it and actively strive to attain it. . . .

When you go to Mass and you recall that you have been unjust to someone, . . . you cannot simply walk into church as though nothing were wrong. For then you would be entering only the physical room of the building, not the congregation, which would not receive you, as you destroy it by your mere presence. . . .

Anyone who knows that somewhere someone has something against him . . . can promise himself to remove the injustice by correcting it as soon as possible. The honest intention suffices to bring down the wall between himself and his "brother." Immediately the unifying element is free again to contact all parts. As soon as the injustice that isolates has been overcome, the congregation is restored. . . .

[Or] you are the one with the complaint. Now you can act much more directly. For the essential depends not on the actual agreement reached by the estranged parties, but on one condition: your forgiveness. As long as you bear your grudge, no matter how "valid," there can be no true congregation as far as you are concerned. Forgive, honestly and sincerely, and the sacred unifying circle will close again. Perhaps this is impossible all at once. Sometimes disappointment and revolt are too great to permit genuine forgiveness right away. Then forgive as much as is in your power and ask God to give you an increase of forgiveness. . . .

Human forgiveness is different from that which the Lord meant. It could be mere prudence, which says, "Let it go—nothing will come of it anyway"; or indifference: "What does it matter?"; or false friendliness, which is no more than inverted dislike; or cowardice, which does not trust itself to fight it out, and so forth. The forgiveness of Christ . . . means that divine love gains a footing in us, creating that new order which is meant to reign among the sons and daughters of God. Hence when you try to fulfill the law of love for the sake of God and His holy mysteries, you make it possible for God to allow the congregation of those rooted in His love to flower.

Romano Guardini
Twentieth century

L ITURGY and justice go together because they are both going in the same direction: Godward. The Christian vision does not allow for pulling in two directions, one vertical and the other horizontal. In Christ these opposites are reconciled. Henceforth there is movement only in one direction: toward God our future.

Mark Searle
Twentieth century

S ABBATH is not only doing no-thing, not only rest and cessation from work . . . Sabbath also includes *recreation in community*. This is the freedom where Jubilee challenges the artistic imagination to the vocation of repairing the world.

Rabbi Marc Gellman offers a midrash (a story about a story in the Bible) on creation that he calls "Partners" as a way of exploring what recreation means. The midrash begins with the angels asking God to clean up the chaos that preceded creation, and after each major creative work—stars, oceans, four-legged animals—the angels ask God whether the world is finished yet. Regularly, God answers, "Nope." Eventually, God makes a woman and a man and says to them, "Please finish up the world for me. I'm tired now and really, it's almost done."

The man and woman at first resist this request, saying to God, "We can't do that. You have the plans and we are too little." So God agrees to a deal where if they keep trying to finish the world, God will be their partner. This divine-human partnership is described in the midrash as "finishing the world," but it is actually the work of repair and recreation to which the ending century challenges and for which Jubilee frees God's people. Sabbath is in the center of this freedom, meaning as it does that having contemplated the Creator of the world, we take up the vocation of recreating, repairing, and finishing it once the Sabbath is over.

Maria Harris
Twentieth century

PEACEMAKING is a life-death struggle. Jesus, the Eucharistic Lamb of God, makes that point unmistakenly clear. We Christians are nourished by his Eucharistic life to enter into that struggle wholeheartedly with all its demands. As militarization increases around this planet earth in ways that have already been characterized as madness and insanity, the Christian response cannot be anything less than all-out efforts for peace even to the point of martyrdom. Our Eucharistic prayer must take on the fullness of global impact and responsibility in our lives. How else can we pray sincerely, "Peace be with you"?

Carol Frances Jegen
Twentieth century

IT would be pointless to do what we do on Sundays if we failed to integrate it with the rest of life. This, in fact, is the commission we are given as the community is dismissed at the end of the liturgy: the commission to integrate the saving reality we have celebrated into the everydayness of our lives. In the words of a Zen master: "Everyday life is the path." This commissioning at the end of Mass echoes the commission given to the women by Jesus on the first day of the week: "Go, tell the brothers the news of my rising. Tell them, I go before you into Galilee" (Matthew 28:10). Galilee, of course, was home for most of them: it was familiar territory, the place where they lived and worked. Like Jesus, they had come from Galilee and had brought with them their peculiar accent and the experience of growing up and working there. Jesus spoke to them in terms of what they knew of life: of marriage and childbirth, of farmers and fishermen, of death and taxes.

Our going up to Jerusalem for worship, for the experience of the dead and risen one, is likewise shaped by what our experience in Galilee has taught us, by what we have learned back home. What we bring to worship is what we experience every day. Fr. Ed Hayes of Kansas City uses the homely analogy of the potluck supper: it is what we bring to the liturgy that makes the occasion feast or famine. What we bring to the liturgy out of our week of living and working and preparing can enhance and challenge what we celebrate. In short, what we all bring to the liturgy is important for the impact it has upon us: it is a matter of being fully present—we, the assembly, Christ the Lord.

Conversely, the space between Sunday and Sunday is a space in which the word must be allowed to take flesh in the everydayness of our lives. If the word is really taken to heart, it will become the radical truth that bespeaks itself in the attitude we adopt towards everyday events. Really, it is a matter of Christian integrity. If we do not live out at home the "Amen" we pronounce in church, what does it mean to be a disciple of the Lord and of his Gospel? We must get to know the word, be confronted by it, struggle with its meaning, surrender to its transforming power.

Benedicta Boland
Twentieth century

Wﾟ

WITH what shall I come before the LORD,
  and bow myself before God on high?
Shall I come before him with burnt offerings,
  with calves a year old?
Will the LORD be pleased with thousands of rams,
  with ten thousands of rivers of oil?
Shall I give my firstborn for my transgression,
  the fruit of my body for the sin of my soul?
He has told you, O mortal, what is good;
  and what does the LORD require of you
but to do justice, and to love kindness,
  and to walk humbly with your God?   Micah 6:6–8

THE Sabbath wisely begins its work on us by engaging our physical senses as a way of quieting our mind. Sabbath time is . . . a feast of pleasures and sensations. The journey from work to rest, from action to Sabbath, is first felt in the body. During Sabbath time we sing with our mouths, we pray with our hands, we light candles, we smell the spices, we eat warm bread, we touch one another as we give and receive our blessings. It is a delight of the senses. . . .

Walk leisurely, don't drive; walk in the garden, don't answer the phone, turn off the television and the radio, forget the CD and the computer. Quiet the insidious technology, and remember that we live in bodies that, through a feast of the senses, appreciate the beauty of the world. Walk under the stars and moon. Knock on the door, don't ring. Sing at the table. Eat, drink, touch, smell, and remember who you are.

Wayne Muller
Twentieth century

THE command to keep holy the Sabbath is therefore a command to strive constantly toward an ideal which is not realized merely in "doing" or even in "doing for" but which finds perfection only in "being with." To keep the Sabbath is to be sensitized to the personal dimension of life; it is to be with others in a personal way, i.e. in a loving, listening, supporting way. It is to be like Jesus.

Demetrius Dumm
Twentieth century

GOOD Sabbaths are times to remember the ancient texts and to think about them in a contemporary context. They are a time to sing. They are a time to forget about ourselves. A time to be quiet together. A time for filtered light. A time for lit candles. A time for preludes and postludes, marked beginnings and endings. Sabbath is a time to let go of the past, to receive a blessing, to be reminded that it is possible to go on. Sabbath is a time to learn more about the core of the universe. It is a time to be in sanctuary, safe space, to look out the windows and know we are safe inside.

Donna Schaper
Twentieth century

N o man can exist without pleasure," remarked St. Thomas Aquinas, who ought—if our understanding of the dour medieval mind is correct—to have been urging us to put away our playthings in favor of prayer. "Life would not be tolerable without poetry," announced Saint Teresa of Avila, making it perfectly clear, in a parenthetical remark, that she meant it would not be tolerable even in a convent for contemplatives. Saint Augustine thought that whenever a conflict arose between the enjoyable and the useful, the useful had to give way as being, in the ultimate sense, inferior. Many of the soberer thinkers of the past, including those who had by vow denied themselves most earthly pleasures, did not scruple to elevate what they called recreation to a dizzying position in the hierarchy of the worth-while. Indeed, "worth-while" is an inadequate word to describe the value they placed upon pleasure. . . . Life would not be tolerable, without such patently superior experiences. . . .

We have achieved a high degree of skill in one kind of groping, the hard kind, the theoretical kind. Our futures now depend upon a most attractive activity: upon our developing a matching skill in the easy kind, the loving kind, the arm-in-arm kind. Praiseworthy as we are in the work we have been doing, and certain as it is that more work will have to be done, our freedom to grow in stature rests unconditionally upon our ability to play. To keep our minds supple and the universe in focus, we are requested, most cordially, to exercise just those intellectual instincts which tend—in their contemplative listening and their intuitive rejoicing—to produce pleasure.

Walter Kerr
Twentieth century

T HE Sabbath rest brings to a halt the creative stream of the week, but it is more than a moment of relaxation: it is a time of inner activity. The authentic expression of menuhah, rest, requires the individual and the community to direct the strength of work's creativity not on the world, but to the spiritual and intellectual dimensions. The creative energies are not suspended but suffer a certain transformation. The object of the creative power is the inner world of the spirit. The Sabbath is a day of inner meeting, of self-discovery, a time to restore individual integrity after a week of work and alienation. The Sabbath allows for a recovery of self out of the routine of weekday involvement.

The Sabbath liturgy speaks of a phenomenon peculiar to the Sabbath: each one receives on that day a "neshamah yeterah," an additional soul, a spiritual dimension that requires cultivation and creative self-search. It is "nomesh," self-transformation, an inner silence that transforms self in depth and meaning. The weekday is devoted to work, creative work for the religious person, but the Sabbath is a time of inner creativity and transformation.

Leon Klenicki
Twentieth century

O*H, look,* old Galileo whispered, *look, we move.*
And burning, burning in the sky, the sun stood still.
Earth turned and spun and whirled about the ball,
but no one else believed. Not then. *Take time,*

Grandfather called, watching our first adopted toddler fall,
push up and waddle to my lap. *It goes so fast.*
Yeah, yeah, I thought, patting my daughter's goldilocks,
thumbing her tears away. I loved that chubby cherub

with the grapejuice grin, took turns changing Pampers,
scrubbing that kid in bubble baths, giving time
and horsey rides, a thousand tasks each day before I slept.
I accuse myself, I confess I doubted that old man.

Walt McDonald
Twentieth century

EVERY Sunday afternoon at 2 PM there is a worship service at the nursing home. The pastors in town share the duty, the Lutherans one week, Presbyterians the next, then the Catholics, then the Church of God. The pastors prepare a Bible reading and brief sermon, and church women bring cookies and coffee. It's a popular event with the residents of the home, those who are mentally alert and those who are less so. I always find it absurdly joyful, a restorative to the soul, but I don't attend as often as I'd like.

What I love most about services is the Lord's Prayer and the singing. It reinforces my belief in the power of poetry, and also in the aptness of Auden's definition of it as "memorable speech." People who may remember little else can still say all the words of the Lord's Prayer (the King James version they grew up with), and they also have a remarkable ability to recall the words of hymns. The last time I conducted the service there—our minister was out of town, and had asked me to fill in—we sang "Stand Up, Stand Up for Jesus," "Blessed Assurance," and "Amazing Grace." One woman would not stop singing "Amazing Grace," so we just let her go happily on, eyes closed, smiling and swaying in her wheelchair, while I said a prayer and a benediction. A pastor later told me that "Holy, Holy, Holy" has the same effect on her.

Kathleen Norris
Twentieth century

I have said that he was almost wholly logical; but not quite. He had been a Presbyterian and was now an Atheist. He spent Sunday, as he spent most of his time on weekdays, working in his garden. But one curious trait from his Presbyterian youth survived. He always, on Sundays, gardened in a different, and slightly more respectable, suit. An Ulster Scot may come to disbelieve in God, but not to wear his weekday clothes on the Sabbath.

C. S. Lewis
Twentieth century

FAMILIES and clans staked out picnic areas and occasional incursive tables within other areas. Sunday peace ruled; lack of war was the tradition between nationalities at Huntington Park. Italians were making spaghetti, Jews were making salads and slicing meats, some of the Irish were making whoopee. The rich brought ice chests. Puffed cheeks blew on charcoal to get things started in the WPA grates. Class distinctions made little difference among fire-starters, though there were isolated instances of kerosene. For a while mother, in her black cotton bathing dress with the modest flap of skirt, came down to the beach to watch my brother and me bobbing on the whitecaps of Lake Erie. She wrinkled her nose. "What kind of smell is that? What kind of fish?"

"Inner tube," I said.

She checked invisible Canada out there. She checked the sky for cloud or storm. She had asked a lifeguard and, although he was a goy, believed him—no sharks in Lake Erie. . . .

Her spirit took a relax in the peace of the Christian sabbath. We would keep an eye on each other, she decided, we had friends, we would take care not to walk out toward Canada where the water got deep. . . . A careful review of all the facts allowed her to go back to fix lunch. Now there was a subject which deeply engaged her.

The noon whistle blew. . . . Regretfully we left the sand spit, my brother and I. We could imagine potato salad and sliced tomatoes and tunafish, also cold pot roast with horse radish and pickles. . . . Swimming, jumping waves, and making contact with new close friends and their Goodyear inner tubes were a few of the basic causes of appetite. I promised a wiry Protestant to return to the beach in half an hour. Sid asked a responsible Catholic to guard the sand city they were building together and to keep the animals from running through it. . . . My brother wanted to bet with me—the fruit Jell-O would be melted. "What's melt?" I asked him. "How soft is melt?"

Our picnic table was piled with goodies. . . . "Oh-ho, have I got something good for you," mother said, as if we didn't know.

Herbert Gold
Twentieth century

DELLA and I have been following an exciting serial in the movies and father lets us go only on Sunday afternoons when it's rainy, but never at any other time during the week. . . . Every day belongs to God and every day we are to serve Him doing His pleasure. And "as every good gift is prepared for them that love God," and moving pictures are a good thing, if you stop to think of the educational advantages of them, therefore, I can see nothing wrong in going to a show and pleasing Della and incidentally myself.

Dorothy Day
Twentieth century

THIS time is given to me by God that I may live in it. It is not given to make something *out of it* but given me to be stored away in eternity as my own.

Thomas Merton
Twentieth century

THERE was a time when I wondered why more people did not go to church. Taken purely as a human recreation, what could be more delightful, more unexpected than to enter a venerable and lavishly scaled building kept warm and clean for use one or two hours a week and to sit and stand in unison and sing and recite creeds and petitions that are like paths worn smooth in the raw terrain of our hearts? To listen, or not listen, as a poorly paid but resplendently robed man strives to console us with scraps of ancient epistles and halting accounts, hopelessly compromised by words, of those intimations of divine joy that are like pain in that, their instant gone, the mind cannot remember or believe them; to witness the windows donated by departed patrons and the altar flowers arranged by withdrawn hands and the whole considered spectacle lustrous beneath its patina of inheritance; to pay, for all this, no more than we are moved to give—surely in all democracy there is nothing like it. Indeed, it is the most available democratic experience. We vote less than once a year. Only in church and at the polls are we actually given our supposed value, the soul-unit of one, with its noumenal arithmetic of equality: one equals one equals one.

John Updike
Twentieth century

TODAY I would strongly urge everyone to rediscover Sunday: *Do not be afraid to give your time to Christ!* Yes, let us open our time to Christ, that he may cast light upon it and give it direction. He is the One who knows the secret of time and the secret of eternity, and he gives us "his day" as an ever new gift of his love. The rediscovery of this day is a grace which we must implore, not only so that we may live the demands of faith to the full, but also so that we may respond concretely to the deepest human yearnings. Time given to Christ is never time lost, but is rather time gained, so that our relationships and indeed our whole life may become more profoundly human.

S OME old men came to see Abba Poemen and said to him, 'When we see brothers who are dozing at the *synaxis,* shall we rouse them so that they will be watchful?' He said to them, 'For my part when I see a brother who is dozing, I put his head on my knees and let him rest.'

I T will not do to fulminate against partying, late television-viewing, or sports-watching. People profit little from being told what isn't good for them. Besides, who is to say? After a week of hassles, the average family person craves a little undisciplined release. For many, nothing fills the bill quite so well as a bash of receptivity, the more passive the better.

The question is, does our present way of spending Sunday qualify as the problem or the solution? It seems to so many that the latter is true that saying the opposite will convince no one. People know that they've earned their rest—often a euphemism for exhausting inactivity. They gravitate toward this with so little encouragement that pressing Sunday rest upon them as the solution to their Sunday problem will strike them as selling bathing suits to Eskimos. Yet Sunday rest is probably what is needed more than anything else if attempts at eucharistic prayer on Sunday are to bear fruit. . . .

The Sabbath rest of Jews on which Christian Sunday rest should be modeled is above all restorative. It has nothing to do with restricted pleasures. . . . Sunday rest is not a matter of what may not be done. It is a matter of what can and should be done. . . .

The problem is so deep-seated that it has to be tackled corporately. . . .

Jewish Sabbath observance or Amish or Mennonite practice is a possibility because people decide to resist the prevailing moods and trends together. But first they must identify a good so important to them that the struggle is worth the effort. *The Christian good regarding the Sunday rest is being made whole in the company of others. . . .* To speak in this way is to propose no less than a cultural revolution. . . .

That will take time. That will take study. . . . It must all begin with some deep reflection on what it means to go back to Eden for a weekly visit, to be in touch with one another in a non-frenetic way, to have a care for the earth after six days of treading on it, punishing, and plundering it.

Gerard S. Sloyan
Twentieth century

COME, let us join with one accord
In hymns around the throne!
This is the day our rising Lord
Hath made and called His own.

This is the day which God hath blest,
The brightest of the sev'n,
Type of that everlasting rest
The saints enjoy in heav'n.

Then let us in His name sing on,
And hasten to that day
When our Redeemer shall come down,
And shadows pass away.

Not one, but all our days below,
Let us in hymns employ;
And in our Lord rejoicing, go
To His eternal joy.

Charles Wesley
Eighteenth century

AT first, eucharist was celebrated after nightfall on Saturday. But eventually, evening meetings of all sorts were outlawed. The eucharist was moved to Sunday morning. In the Roman Empire, Sunday was a work day. Saturday—at least in Jewish territories—was the day of rest; Sunday was business as usual. But for Christians, that business as usual was transformed because of the morning eucharist, and every task done on Sunday became an opportunity to bring the reign of God closer to completion.

Today, many of us again work on Sundays. This is unfortunate because it robs us of leisure that we need to live differently this day, to dream about the world the way that it could be and to prepare ourselves to try again to make it so. But drawing on the experience of the first Christians, those of us who work this day can keep Sunday holy by dedicating our labor to the coming of God's reign. Practice finding God in signs of creation, resurrection and re-creation. Give thanks for God's goodness in the produce aisle of the market. Be Christ's healing hand in the nursing home. Hear the Spirit's coming as the laundry rustles on the clothesline, and smell the coming of the reign of God in bread rising in the oven. Breathe Christ's peace to those you encounter on your patrol.

For those of us who do not work on Sunday, let's resolve to keep the Day of the Lord and the Day of the Church as gracious stewards of holy time. . . .

Remember that this day is practice for eternity. And when it comes to an end, when the shift is over, the dinner dishes done, the sun set, lift up your hearts again to God, and give thanks and praise for this moment of heaven on earth and this promise of earth becoming heaven, this Sunday that God has given us.

David Philippart
Twentieth century

I am about to do a new thing;
   now it springs forth, do you not perceive it?
I will make a way in the wilderness
   and rivers in the desert.

I give water in the wilderness,
   rivers in the desert,
to give drink to my chosen people,
   the people whom I formed for myself
so that they might declare my praise.

Isaiah 43:19, 20b, 21b

THE sad fact is that we do ignore sabbath rest—we who probably need it most. We have created a week even the pagan Romans wouldn't recognize, without any day off, without any sort of sabbath.

Recall that we are commanded by the Most High to keep the sabbath in grateful remembrance for our liberation from slavery. But how can liberation be celebrated if we spend our "free" time in apparent subservience? A sabbath cannot happen until people learn that it's OK to spend a day doing nothing at all—like the Creator, like the Redeemer.

A day of rest can happen only through self-discipline in homes, in households, in agreements (and even in a few arguments) among employers and employees, among family and community members. Those who would wear the crown of the sabbath are those who recognize the dignity to which they are called. Those who would receive this gift from God are those who spend their lives working for the reign of God at work and at rest.

Peter Mazar
Twentieth century

THE angel stood by the tomb, and cried aloud to the myrrh-bearing woman: myrrh is fitting for the dead, but Christ has shown himself a stranger to corruption. Cry out instead: Christ is risen granting great mercy to the world.

Orthodox liturgy

SUNDAY is a time not only for relaxing but also for literally regenerating our culture. It is a time for reminding ourselves that we have children to care for and that we have a history to celebrate. . . . We use a variety of symbols—children, nostalgia, family memories, scrapbooks—and a variety of other stimuli to remind us that we are a part of a human chain that extends back into history and forward into the future. There is a mystical quality of being a part of all that has lived and all that will live which seems to be available to us in these moments of reflecting on the regenerative properties of our culture. Sunday seems to be a unique time when those symbols are available to us.

William C. McCready
Twentieth century

IT is quite disgraceful that the pagans who do not know the faith of Christ, but worship idols and demons, should honor the day of Jupiter or any other demon and abstain from work, when demons certainly never created and do not have any day. Yet we, who worship the true God and believe that the Son of God rose from the dead, do not honor the day of the resurrection, the Lord's Day. Do not do wrong to the resurrection of the Lord, but honor it and hold it in reverence for the sake of the hope which we have in it. For just as He, our Lord Jesus Christ, the Son of God, who is our Head, rose from the dead on the third day, so, too, do we hope that we who are His members shall rise in our flesh at the end of the world.

Martin of Braga
Sixth century

THE God who made the Sabbath is not a cranky schoolmaster, always forbidding, coercing obedience, and watching sniveling subjects slinking about in cowardly compliance. The Sabbath commandment comes from a kind, wise teacher who does not like to see us suffer. Let me make it easier for you, God says. Some things at first may seem expedient, or important, or profitable—but in the end, they will bring you suffering. If you work all week and forget to rest, you will become brittle and hard, and lose precious nourishment and joy. Forgetting the Sabbath is like forgetting to unwrap the most beautiful gift under the tree.

If we forget to rest we will work too hard and forget our more tender mercies, forget those who we love, forget our children and our natural wonder. God says: Please, don't. It is a waste of a tremendous gift I have given you. If you knew the value of your life, you would not waste a single breath. So I give you this commandment: Remember to rest. This is not a lifestyle suggestion, but a commandment—as important as not stealing, not murdering, or not lying. Remember to play and bless and make love and eat with those you love, and take comfort, easy and long, in this gift of sacred rest.

Wayne Muller
Twentieth century

As the new century dawns, the practice of Sabbath keeping may be a gift just waiting to be unwrapped, a confirmation that we are not without help in shaping the renewing ways of life for which we long. . . .

Unwrapping this gift . . . requires supporting *underworked* Americans as they wonder what Sabbath keeping might mean for them. One of the cruelest features of the American economy, which asks too much of many people, is that it casts numerous others aside, leaving them without sufficient work. A Sabbath-keeping community . . . would be a community in which this injustice would not occur. When Sabbath comes, commerce halts, feasts are served, and all Gods' children play. The equal reliance of all people on the bounty and grace of God is gratefully acknowledged, and the goodness of weekday work is affirmed. Relationships that persist throughout the week are changed in the process. As the great Jewish scholar Abraham Joshua Heschel said, "The Sabbath cannot survive in exile, a lonely stranger among days of profanity."

Dorothy C. Bass
Twentieth century

WHAT stood will stand, though all be fallen.
The good return that time has stolen.
Though creatures groan in misery,
Their flesh prefigures liberty
To end travail and bring to birth
Their new perfection in new earth.
At word of that enlivening
Let the trees of the wood all sing
And every field rejoice, let praise
Rise up out of the ground like grass.
What stood, whole in every piecemeal
Thing that stood, will stand though all
Fall—field and woods and all in them
Rejoin the primal Sabbath's hymn.

Wendell Berry
Twentieth century

ON the sabbath everyone without exception was commanded to do no work and to rest, inactive. Why then did the Lord break the sabbath by saying: "Have you not read in the law how the priests on temple duty can break the Sabbath rest without incurring guilt?". . . .

Great, indeed, are the works of God: he holds the sky in his hands, and he gives light to the sun and other planets, gives growth to the plants of the earth, maintains man in life. . . . Yes, everything in heaven and on earth has its being and lives through the will of God the Father; everything comes from God, and everything exists through the Son. He is, in fact, the head and the principle of all things. In him everything was made. And it is out of the fullness contained in himself, according to the initiative of his eternal power, that he has created everything.

If Christ is active in all things, it follows that it is the Father's action which acts in Christ. That is why he said: "My Father is at work until now, and I am at work as well." Because all that Christ does, as the Son of God indwelt by God the Father, is the work of the Father. Thus everything in each day is created by the Son. Thus, Christ's action goes on every day; and, it seems to me, the principles of life, the formation of bodies, and the development and growth of living things manifest this action. . . .

Does God then work on the sabbath? He certainly does; otherwise the sky would disappear, the light of the sun would go out, the earth would fall apart, all its fruits would dry up, and the life of man would perish if, because of the sabbath, the moving power of the universe were to stop working. But in fact there is no cessation: during the sabbath, just as during the other six days, the elements of the universe continue to fulfil their function. For through them the Father is working now and always.

But he acts in the Son who is begotten of him and through whom everything is his work. . . . For through the Son the Father's action goes on during the sabbath. And consequently there is no rest for God since there is no day that sees the cessation of God's works.

So it is with God's action. But what of his rest? God's work is Christ's work. And God's rest is God, Christ, because all that pertains to God is truly in Christ to such a degree that the Father can find rest in him.

Hilary of Poitiers
Fourth century

IT would be banal to interpret God's "rest" as a kind of divine "inactivity." By its nature, the creative act which founds the world is unceasing and God is always at work, as Jesus himself declares in speaking of the Sabbath precept: "My Father is working still, and I am working" (John 5:17). The divine rest of the seventh day does not allude to an inactive God, but emphasizes the fullness of what has been accomplished. It speaks, as it were, of God's lingering before the "very good" work (Genesis 1:31) which his hand has wrought in order to cast upon it *a gaze full of joyous delight.* This is a contemplative gaze which does not look to new accomplishments but enjoys the beauty of what has already been achieved. It is a gaze which God casts upon all things, but in a special way upon human beings, the crown of creation. It is a gaze which already discloses something of the nuptial shape of the relationship which God wants to establish with the creature made in his own image, by calling that creature to enter a pact of love. This is what God will gradually accomplish in offering salvation to all humanity through the saving covenant made with Israel and fulfilled in Christ. It will be the Word incarnate, through the eschatological gift of the Holy Spirit and the configuration of the church as his body and bride, who will extend to all humanity the offer of mercy and the call of the Father's love.

Pope John Paul II
Twentieth century

NOW resting, blessed and hallowed the seventh Day,
As resting on that day from all his work;
But not in silence holy kept: the harp
Had work, and rested not; the solemn pipe
And dulcimer, all organs of sweet stop,
All sounds on fret by string or golden wire,
Tempered soft tunings, intermixed with voice
Choral or unison; of incense clouds,
Fuming from golden censers, hid the Mount.
Creation and the Six Days' acts they sung:—
"Great are thy works, Jehovah! infinite
Thy power! what thought can measure thee, or tongue
Relate thee—greater now in thy return

Than from the Giant-angels? Thee that day
Thy thunders magnified; but to create
Is greater than created to destroy.
Who can impair thee, mighty King, or bound
Thy empire? Easily the proud attempt
Of Spirits apostate, and their counsels vain,
Thou hast repelled, while impiously they thought
Thee to diminish, and from thee withdraw
The number of thy worshipers. Who seeks
To lessen thee, against his purpose, serves
To manifest the more thy might; his evil
Thou usest, and from thence creat'st more good.
Witness this new-made World, another Heaven
From Heaven-gate not far, founded in view
On the clear hyaline, the glassy sea;
Of amplitude almost immense, with stars
Numerous, and every star perhaps a world
Of destined habitation—but thou know'st
Their seasons; among these the seat of men,
Earth, with her nether ocean circumfused,
Their pleasant dwelling-place. Thrice happy men,
And sons of men, who God hath thus advanced,
Created in his image, there to dwell
And worship him, and in reward to rule
Over his works, on earth, in sea, or air,
And multiply a race of worshipers
Holy and just! thrice happy, if they know
Their happiness, and persevere upright!"
    So sung they, and Empyrean rung
With halleluiahs. Thus was Sabbath kept.
And thy request think now fulfilled, that asked
How first this World and face of things began,
And what before thy memory was done
From the beginning, that posterity,
Informed by thee, might know. If else thou seek'st
Aught, not surpassing human measure, say.

John Milton
Seventeenth century

IN the beginning, the spirit-wind of God moves across the face of the deep. The deep is not barren but pregnant, an emptiness teeming with the promise of life. Rabbi Zalman Schachter-Shalomi suggests a more accurate reading of the Hebrew would be "In a beginning," as if there were endless beginnings in the cycle of life. Biblical scholars also agree that the phrase "God created" would be better translated "when God *began to create.*" So the story literally begins: *In a beginning, when God began to create the heavens and the earth. . . .*

Creation, then, is an ongoing story of new beginnings, opportunities to begin again and again. God began to create, is still creating; nothing is finished. Creation continues to arise out of emptiness, take form, and dissolve over time, dust to dust, returning to emptiness. All life arises and falls away in this beautiful, fruitful rhythm.

Later, in the book of Exodus, we read, "In six days God made heaven and earth, and on the seventh day God rested, and was refreshed." Here, the word "refreshed," *vaiynafesh,* literally means, *and God exhaled.* The creation of the world was like the life-quickening inhale; the Sabbath is the exhale. Thus, in a beginning, all creation moves with the rhythm of the inhale and the exhale. Without the Sabbath exhale, the life-giving inhale is impossible.

Wayne Muller
Twentieth century

YOU cause the grass to grow for the cattle,
   and plants for people to use,
to bring forth food from the earth,
   and wine to gladden the human heart,
oil to make the face shine,
   and bread to strengthen the human heart.
The trees of the LORD are watered abundantly,
   the cedars of Lebanon that he planted.
In them the birds build their nests,
the stork has its home in the fir trees.
The high mountains are for the wild goats;
   the rocks are a refuge for the coneys.

You have made the moon to mark the seasons;
   the sun knows its time for setting.
You make darkness, and it is night,
   when all the animals of the forest come creeping out.
The young lions roar for their prey,
   seeking their food from God.
When the sun rises, they withdraw
   and lie down in their dens.
People go out to their work
   and to their labor until the evening.
O LORD, how manifold are your works!
   In wisdom you have made them all;
the earth is full of your creatures.

Psalm 104:14–24

BUT you, Lord, always work and are always at rest. You do not see things in time, nor are you moved in time, nor do you rest in time, and yet you make things that are seen in time, yes, you make time itself and the rest which results from time.

We, therefore, see these things which you made, because they really exist, but they exist only because you see them. And we see around us that they really are, and see inside us that they are good, but you saw them already finished exactly where you saw them before they were ever made. And we were at a later time moved to do good things after our hearts had conceived these good things through your spirit. In earlier times, forsaking you, we were moved to do evil, but you, our one God, our good God, never ceased to do good. We also have some good works to our credit, your gifts to us, but not eternal ones. After them we hope to rest in your great hallowing. But you, being the good which needs no good, are ever at rest, because your rest is in you yourself. What man can teach another man to understand this? Or what angel teach another angel? Or what angel, a man? Let it be asked of you, sought in you, knocked for at your door. Thus shall it be received, thus shall it be found, thus shall it be opened.

*Saint Augustine
Fifth century*

MY ego is like a fortress.
I have built its walls stone by stone
To hold out the invasion of the love of God.
But I have stayed here long enough. There is light
Over the barriers. O My God—
The darkness of my house forgive
And overtake my soul.
I relax the barriers.
I abandon all that I think I am,
All that I hope to be,
All that I believe I possess.
I let go of the past,
I withdraw my grasping hand from the future,
And in the great silence of this moment,
I alertly rest my soul.
As the sea gull lays in the wind current,
So I lay myself in the spirit of God.
My dearest human relationships,
My most precious dreams,
I surrender to His care.
All that I have called my own
I give back. All my favorite things
Which I would withhold in my storehouse
From his fearful tyranny,
I let go.
I give myself
Unto Thee, O my God.

Howard Thurman
Twentieth century

CEASING labor is the way that human beings can carry out
the first element in the Sabbath command: "Remember."
Remember that God's world is not a place of endless productivity, ambition, or anxiety. Instead, it is a place where
listening to and receiving word and world precede our tend-
ing to them.

Phrased and translated in the form of a negative injunction (You shall stop; You shall cease), . . . revealed as a mystical not-doing. . . .

The strictness and importance of the Sabbath command to stop, to cease work, and to not-do are borne out by the fact that its rigorous observance is enjoined in all of the biblical decalogues that constitute what is essential for covenant: Exodus 20:2–17; 20:23–24; 34:21; and Deuteronomy 5:6–18. The utter seriousness of the Sabbath command reverberates centuries later—in Protestantism, in the form of restrictions in Puritan and Scottish Sabbath teaching, and in Catholicism, in the form of sanctions against absence from Sunday Eucharist that declared the absentee guilty of serious sin. Even when these commands seem overstrict, they nonetheless bear out the intuition that Sabbath must never be taken lightly. . . .

. . . Despite being the ritually observed sacrament of God's presence, Sabbath was never entirely ceremonial; a conviction that also shapes the Jubilee. Instead, from early in its promulgation, Sabbath included the regular practice of justice. It was an ethical and moral teaching as well as a liturgical rite, a statement about human beings' relations with other humans (spouse, children, enslaved and indentured workers, strangers). It extended much further than the human community, however. Sabbath also assumed concern for other animals and the earth: the four-leggeds, the winged ones, the gilled ones once again. And only then, when the ceremonial and the ethical were in place, did the command to *stop* become transformed into the command to *rest*.

As such, Sabbath becomes a time for genuine listening and for the recollection in tranquility that listening makes possible. As we welcome the Sabbath of full and complete rest, often referred to as "bride Sabbath," we can cultivate the second soul, or *neshamah yeterah,* given to everyone during it. We can become attentive to the suffering and the pain in the world. . . . And we can meditate on the implications in our own lives for what the rabbis refer to as the unity of devotion and deed; the marriage of what is real and what is to be realized; and the coming together of the world of mystery with the world of commandment.

Maria Harris
Twentieth century

THE LOON ON OAK-HEAD POND

cries for three days, in the gray mist.
cries for the north it hopes it can find.

plunges, and comes up with a slapping pickerel.
blinks its red eye.

cries again.

you come every afternoon, and wait to hear it.
you sit a long time, quiet, under the thick pines,
in the silence that follows.

as though it were your own twilight.
as though it were your own vanishing song.

Mary Oliver
Twentieth century

OBVIOUSLY, the ancient rabbis concluded, there was an act of creation on the seventh day. Just as heaven and earth were created in six days, *menuha* was created on the Sabbath. . . .

Menuha which we usually render with "rest" means here much more than withdrawal from labor and exertion, more than freedom from toil, strain or activity of any kind. *Menuha* is not a negative concept but something real and intrinsically positive. This must have been the view of the ancient rabbis if they believed that it took a special act of creation to bring it into being, that the universe would be incomplete without it. . . .

To the biblical mind *menuha* is the same as happiness and stillness, as peace and harmony. The word with which Job described the state after life he was longing for is derived from the same root as *menuha*. It is the state wherein man lies still, wherein the wicked cease from troubling and the weary are at rest. It is the state in which there is no strife and no fighting, no fear and no distrust. The essence of good life is *menuha*. "The Lord is my shepherd, I shall not want,

Abraham
Joshua Heschel
Twentieth century

He maketh me to lie down in green pastures; He leadeth me beside the still waters" (the waters of *menuhot*). In later times *menuha* became a synonym for the life in the world to come, for eternal life.

CONSIDER the lilies of the field,
the blue banks of camas opening
into acres of sky along the road.
Would the longing to lie down
and be washed by that beauty
abate if you knew their usefulness,
how the natives ground their bulbs
for flour, how the settlers' hogs
uprooted them, grunting in gleeful
oblivion as the flowers fell?

And you—what of your rushed and
useful life? Imagine setting it all down—
papers, plans, appointments, everything—
leaving only a note: "Gone to the fields
to be lovely. Be back when I'm through
with blooming."

Even now, unneeded and uneaten, the
camas lilies gaze out above the grass
from their tender blue eyes.
Even in sleep your life will shine.
Make no mistake.
Of course
your work will always matter.
Yet Solomon in all his glory
was not arrayed like one of these.

Lynn Ungar
Twentieth century

STOPPING work tests our trust: will the world and I fall apart if I stop making things happen for a while? Is life really gifted and the Spirit moving through it, so that I can truly rest and taste this playful caring? Can I trust that this caring will be the bottom line when I rest, beneath all the suppressed and repressed sides of myself that are likely to rise when I relax my controlling reins? Is there truly a unique image of God in me that is simply given and rises to obscure awareness in such spacious times, an image that is my deepest identity? Or is there really no such deep self in God, and does everything really depend on my producing, asserting, and protecting a conscious, managing ego-self?

The lingering doubts and confusions in us about these different senses of reality necessitate intentional sabbath rest. Such time is an opportunity to pull out of the temptation to collapse ourselves and all meaning into our self-productive world. It is an opportunity to realize our true sanity, wherein we allow trust in the Holy One living before and through us, with whom we weave a unique thread that contributes to the tapestry of the Kingdom's fullness.

Tilden Edwards
Twentieth century

IT would seem that there are certain experiences in the perverse life of ours that will not yield to command; they will yield only to surrender—like Maurice Chevalier's squirrels. M. Chevalier once explained to an interviewer that pleasing an audience in the theater was like feeding hungry squirrels. Mo matter how hungry they might be, you couldn't foist your treats upon them. You couldn't call to them, urge them, make an obvious offer. You had to pretend to an absolute indifference, perhaps even come to feel something like indifference, before you could reach *rapprochement.* Once you'd settled down quietly and seemed to promise nothing, they would come comfortably to you. . . .

Our minds will meet with no profound pleasure until they have ceased being acquisitive. They will never be able to fasten firmly upon the very joys they most desire unless they first show signs of a willingness to let go.

Walter Kerr
Twentieth century

S OMETIMES, when we feel trapped by a problem, we must surrender to not knowing the solution. Sometimes it is only when we let the problem alone, when we back off in unknowing, that it has the space to solve itself.

Edward Gibbon conceived his history of the rise and fall of the Roman Empire while listening to a choir of monks at vespers. Nobel physicist Steven Weinberg was nagged by the problem of how nuclear reactions produce the heat of the sun—until it came to him one day unbidden as he was driving around Boston in his red Camaro. Allegedly, Archimedes discovered the law of specific gravity while taking a bath. Sometimes our greatest wisdom comes when we are not striving to discover anything at all. . . .

Sabbath honors this quality of not knowing, an open receptivity of mind essential for allowing things to speak to us from where they are. If we take a day and rest, we cultivate Sabbath Mind. We let go of knowing what will happen next, and find the courage to wait for the teaching that has not yet emerged. The presumption of the Sabbath is that *it is good,* and that the wisdom, courage, and clarity we need are already embededed in creation. The solution is already alive in the problem. Our work is not always to push and strive and struggle. Sometimes we have only to be still, says the Psalmist, and we will know.

Wayne Muller
Twentieth century

B Y indirections find directions out.

William Shakespeare
Sixteenth century

A FTER the ceasing, the resting, and the embracing comes the feasting.

Marva Dawn
Twentieth century

To eat any meal together is to meet at the level of our most basic need. It is hard to preserve your dignity with butter on your chin or to keep your distance when asking for the tomato ketchup.

Frederick Buechner
Twentieth century

IBI sunt sedilia strata
Et domus veils ornata;
Floresque in domo sparguntur,
Herbaeque fragrantes miscentur.

Est ibi mensa apposita,
Universis cibis onusta;
Ibi clarum vinum abundat
Et quicquid te, cara, delectat.

Ibi sonant dulces symphoniae,
Inflantur et altius tibiae;
Ibi puer et docta puella
Pangunt tibi carmina bella.

There are couches strewn and the house is draped with curtains. Flowers, mingled with sweet-smelling herbs, are scattered through the house.

A table is ready, laden with food of every kind. Sparkling wine is there in abundance, and everything that may give you pleasure, dear.

There sweet symphonies sound and shrill flutes are blown. There a lad and well-trained girl are singing fine songs for you.

The Cambridge Songs
Eleventh century

THE Church needs only priest, people, table, bread and wine; the union of those remains the taproot of all its liturgy. So also with the family. Parents and children, table and food are the fundamental pieces. Given these, there will develop, with absolute inevitability, a way of doing business native to that Board and its distinctive materialities. "At our house, we always have icebox cake on Daddy's birthday."

That is genuine liturgy. The key to its true rationale is the phrase "We always do. . . ." The test of its germaneness is not its conformity to some abstract standard of perfection, but simply whether it constitutes an honest doing of the work of the city with the materials at hand. Liturgy is a local matter: The Church has had almost as many liturgies as she has had altars. . . . And since the family is so utterly local a proposition, its truest liturgies will be home-grown—and very often peculiar, in both senses of the word. They will be wordy or brief, elaborate or plain, high or low, according to the tastes and the talents of the families that will make them. But their constant feature is that they will never fail to be made. The Table is simply the kind of thing that brings them forth.

Robert Farrar Capon
Twentieth century

SOME hae meat and canna eat,
And some wad eat that want it;
But we hae meat, and we can eat,
And sae the Lord be thankit.

Robert Burns
Eighteenth century

EIGHT a.m. Mass would be just a memory and the Omaha World-Herald would be scattered about the living room as we sat down to my mother's pot roast, boiled potatoes and canned vegetables, or chicken, green vegetables, mashed potatoes and salty gravy with cake, pie or canned fruit cocktail for dessert. Dad would retell comic incidents from his job as an electrical engineer for the Omaha Public Power District. My three older sisters or Rob would talk about what our teachers said at school, or what chums did to annoy them or what their schemes were for the afternoon. Mom would talk about the content of phone calls or letters she'd gotten from old friends or relatives. Reaching for a second helping, I'd probably spill my glass of milk. And in that serene, good-natured, Ozzie and Harriet setting we each got a sense of where we'd been, who we were and what we hoped to become. It gave us our identity, not just as a family of two parents and five children, but as unique individuals within that grouping.

Jesus was doing that in all his meals, singling out his hosts and guests as highly individual children of God admonishing, praising or helping them as they needed, and yet generalizing in ways that are instructive to us even today. And that is never more true than in his ascent to Jerusalem and the stunning climax of his Last Supper. There a new paschal mystery is introduced, that of Christ "passing over" to his Father and redeeming creation through his life, death, resurrection, ascension and exaltation. As presented in Luke, the supper is a liturgical event in which Christ offers thanksgiving to God and shares the matzo with his friends, connecting those actions—through the metonymy "body"—with the affliction he will suffer on the Cross.

Ron Hansen
Twentieth century

THE table is, beyond all others, the *social furnishing*. It is, to begin with, the piece of furniture made for reunions; being accessible from all sides, the table is made to be surrounded. . . . Here, then, in the center of a common room, the members of the family have a kind of permanent, though tacit, rendezvous. . . .

As furniture for reunion, the table is also furniture for *dialogue.* Together with chair or bench, the support given by the table enables people to sit in great comfort. The level surface, the upper limbs resting on it, and the chest and face rising above it, all mark out for each sitter a space for his personal gestures and for countless possible actions. The physical relaxation of the posture gives full freedom for reflection and speaking. The faces turn to one another and the gazes meet. The hands, freed from toil, can lend themselves fully to the effort of self-expression. Each person involves himself with all the others and communicates himself in the process. Thus the table is the place beyond all others for dialogue between members of the family.

Edmund Barbotin
Twentieth century

BUBER recounts the tale of an old rabbi, Abraham Yehoshua Heshel, who was considering the prospect of his death. Pushing back from the table after the noon meal, he recited the benediction, then stood up and began to pace slowly. Alone in the room, he pondered with knitted brow what God's verdict would be on his accomplishments. Suddenly his face glowed. Abraham stopped by the table covered with crumbs, reached out and gently stroked it with his hand. "Table, good table," he said, "you will testify on my behalf that I have properly eaten and properly prayed at your board.". . .

Kelton Cobb
Twentieth century

The table blessing is not simply a nice custom. It is a sacramental litany.

BLESSED are you, Lord God, king of the universe:
you raised your beloved Son from the dead,
and made him Lord of all.
We turn to you in prayer
and ask you to bless + us
and this food you have given us.
Help us to be generous toward others,
and to work with them so that they too may eat well.
Loving Father,
may we all celebrate together
around your table in heaven.
We praise you and give you glory
through Christ our Lord.

Canadian Conference
of Catholic Bishops

CHICKEN is traditionally festive in overtone, in spite of everything modern factory farming has achieved in making the bird cheap and constantly available. Barbara Pym's novels are full of sly insights into culinary anthropology; in them, "a bird" is for when clergymen are invited for dinner: elevated, not too fleshly, and with a skin "gold-embroidered like a chasuble," as Proust put it. . . .

European settlers brought to North America the tradition that eating fowl was special—behaviour both ceremonial and festive. Rich families ate roast chicken, shared out by the knife-wielding chief male of the family, on Sundays. King Henri IV of France had in the sixteenth century pronounced the ideal of extending this universally desired luxury to everybody: "I hope to make France so prosperous that every peasant will have a chicken in his pot on Sundays." Americans worked hard to turn the occasional treat into an everyday occurrence, as well as to make it available to all. In 1928 the Republican Party won an election in the United States with the help of the slogan, "A chicken in every pot": even the limitation to periodicity had been broken. As chicken became increasingly common, the role of the roasted festive fowl fell more often to the turkey, which was winged, feathered, and fattened, and could be roasted to an elaborate gold like a chicken, but which was much more impressive in size, with a larger capacity for special stuffings. A whole roast chicken can still exude some of its former stylish glory, however. Indeed, the facts that it is pale meat and perceived as "light" have recently added to its prestige. . . .

In North America, especially in the southern United States, there arose a strong preference for fried chicken: fowl cut up in advance instead of being ceremonially carved the assembled group. Chicken in pieces became one of the original American "finger foods," eaten on occasions where formality is sacrificed to relaxed conviviality.

Margaret Visser
Twentieth century

SUNDAYS and church suppers go together,
even better than collards and ham
and honey-glazed yams,
fried chicken and black-eyed peas,
and pumpkin pie—and I better stop
before my stomach starts to growl.

While pastor preaches,
I can't help but wiggle in my pew.
Some Sundays, it's all I can do
to keep from crisscrossing the floor
and tearing through the door
that leads to the church dining hall.

I check the clock (it's way past noon)
and pray that the service will be over soon,
and sometimes, when it is,
I yell "Amen" louder than anyone there,
and hardly care who hears me,
'cause all I can think about is food!

Nikki Grimes
Twentieth century

YOU can't get good turnip greens," Grandpa said,
    "Now that Big Sam has passed away."
"They're good if you can fix them," Grandma said.
"Don't let the texture boil away."
"You can't just leave them like you do collards."
Mama mixed corn bread in a pan.
"I can't stand no mushy greens, mushy rice
Or a preacher without a plan."
"Mushy old greens and a no-plan preacher!
You got to hook them up one day!"
Grandpa laughed and ducked
    under Grandma's look
And we went on living Sunday.

Walter Dean Myers
Twentieth century

YOU shall also go to the kitchen and see to it
that the provisions for the brothers of the house are
    good enough,
that your thriftiness and the cook's laziness
may not rob our Lord
of sweet song in choir,
for a hungry monk never sings well
and a hungry man cannot study deeply.
Thus might God often lose the best
because of the least.

Mechtild of
Magdeburg
Thirteenth century

JESUS . . . tells us to pray for our daily bread. He tells us
that the kingdom of God is like yeast and that we do not
live by bread alone. The Gospels describe an abundance of
food: Jesus multiplies the loaves and fishes, he changes
water into wine at the marriage feast at Cana, the fishers'
nets fill to the breaking point, and God promises in the
Magnificat to fill the hungry with good things. In the Gospel
stories, Jesus eats simple food by the lake, but he also eats
banquet foods at the feast.

Carol Wesley
Twentieth century

BE present at our table, Lord;
Be here and everywhere adored.
These creatures bless, and grant that we
May feast in paradise with thee.

John Wesley
Eighteenth century

EXODUS 16, the story of the manna in the desert, . . . is
more than a feeding miracle; it is the description of an
alternative to the socioeconomic system that had enslaved
the Hebrews. It rests on the premise that food is a divine
gift and that human beings are stewards of that gift. Then it
gives three defining characteristics of alternative economic

practice: gather only enough bread for the needs of your family, so everyone has enough (in contrast to the system of wealth-and-want accomplished through slavery and oppression); do not hoard; and except for what is needed on the Sabbath, do not store excess bread (wealth and power in the Egypt of the Exodus were defined by surplus accumulation; forced labor was used to build store cities); rest on the Sabbath, abstaining even from cooking and eating (that is, the most basic human activities).

When Exodus 16 is read in conjunction with the jubilee codes in Leviticus, God teaches Israel about its dependence on a land that is God's gift to the people, a gift that must be shared equitably and that is not to be viewed as a possession to exploit. Prescribed rest for the land (literally, letting fields lie fallow) and rest for human labor runs counter to our attempts to control nature and maximize the forces of production. Human life is not measured by its productivity. What a contrast to the insistence that we human beings are only worthwhile as either workers or consumers! No wonder the Israelites were also told to keep a jarful of manna in front of the covenant (Exodus 16:33), as a reminder of human dependence upon the divine economy of grace.

Marie Dennis
Twentieth century

Guillermo, native of
Balearic Islands, Spain
Twentieth century

THERE is always enough, and enough is plenty.

I said to Wes Jackson that an economy based on energy would be more comprehensive than an economy based on money.

"But that would still not be comprehensive enough."

"What economy would be comprehensive enough?"

He said, after a pause: "The kingdom of God."
His allusion, I assume, was to the economics of St. Matthew 6:31–33.

Wendell Berry
Twentieth century

THE gesture of a gift is adequate.
If you have nothing: laurel leaf or bay,
no flower, no seed, no apple gathered late,
do not in desperation lay
the beauty of your tears upon the clay.

No gift is proper to a Deity;
no fruit is worthy for such power to bless.
If you have nothing, gather back your sigh,
and with your hands held high, your heart held high,
lift up your emptiness!

Jessica Powers
Twentieth century

FIND a spot and sit there
until the grass begins
to nose between your thighs.

Climb to the top
of a pine and drink
the wind's green breath.

Track the stream through alder and scrub,
trade speech
for that cold sweet babble.

Gather sticks and spin them into fire.
Watch the smoke spiral into darkness.
Dream that the animals find you.

They weave your hair into warm cloth,
string your teeth on necklaces,
wrap your skin soft around their feet.

Wake to the silence
of your own scattered bones.
Watch them whiten in the sun.

When they have fallen to powder
and blown away,
the land will be yours.

Morgan Farley
Twentieth century

LOOK, it is obvious that we have a very easy life. The grass grows by itself, the animals reproduce by themselves, they give milk and meat without our doing anything. So how can you say our way of life is hard?

Nomad of Chang
Tang, Tibet
Twentieth century

WHAT is impractical and unsustainable is the current global scale of greed, and most of us know it. We just don't take the spiritual risk of living as though that were true.

We need to redefine supply and demand for a new Sabbath economic. As John Henry Cardinal Newman has said, the real task of the university is "not to supply people to meet an existing demand but to create the sort of people who create a new sort of demand."

An economic program I could sign up for would slowly reduce—or humanize—the so-called American standard of living. . . . If we go for more, instead of less, we only hurt ourselves. Terribly. Even as we do every day right now, rushing, rushing from page to page. We structure the injustice more deeply. . . . The goal of globalization is more. Do you really want to be the head of the world's body? Do you really want the rest of the world to be your muscles? Can you bear that injustice-masquerading-as-necessity?

Donna Schaper
Twentieth century

JESUS of the wedding feast, of breakfast by the lake, bless this food we have prepared for you and all our friends. Be with us now and at all our meals, give us appetite and joy in eating together. Blessed be God for our daily bread.

A New Zealand
Prayer Book

THEY said to him, "Rabbi" (which translated means Teacher), "where are you staying?" He said to them, "Come and see." They came and saw where he was staying, and they remained with him that day.

John 1:38b

WHAT an aspect of comfort did his houseplace present, after her humble cellar. She did not think of comparing; but for all that she felt the delicious glow of the fire, the savoury smells, the comfortable sounds of a boiling kettle, and the hissing, frizzling ham. With a little old-fashioned curtsey she shut the door, and replied with a loving heart to the boisterous and surprised greeting of her brother.

Elizabeth Gaskell
Nineteenth century

A Catholic priest recently told a gathering of friends about a time when he arrived in Israel late on a Friday afternoon, just as everything was about to shut down for the Sabbath. Public transportation was no longer available, and the house where people were expecting him was fifteen miles away. So he picked up his suitcase and started to walk. He did not get far before a family saw him and invited him to spend the Sabbath with them. He accepted their invitation, and they all had a wonderful time. When Saturday evening came, he found his bus and went on his way.

After the priest finished his story, a Jewish friend said that he had a similar story to tell. As a long-haired college student in the late 1960's, he was traveling through Spain. One night, he got off a train in a village that was already asleep. A little frightened, he approached the only lighted place. It turned out to be a monastery, and the monks received him gladly. After his departure, he discovered that they had quietly slipped some coins into his pocket as he slept.

In both of these stories, we get glimpses of ancient traditions sustaining ways of life that shelter and nourish people, ways of life ready to receive strangers who are passing through. The hospitality these two young men received came from communities structured with hospitality in mind. In each of these places, hospitality was more than an individual act of kindness—it was sustained by a way of life.

What would happen in our society today if young men like these were wandering through? Perhaps they would be fortunate and find a safe place to rest. But they, or others not so different from them, might not. For is there not a crisis of hospitality in our society? It is tragically evident in homelessness and widespread hostility to immigrants. But it affects almost everyone in less noticeable ways as well. A stranger smiles, and we cautiously turn away. In our retreat from hospitality, we find that even friends and relatives sit at our tables less often than they used to. . . .

The shared ways of life that sustain hospitality are changing all around us.

Craig Dykstra and
Dorothy C. Bass
Twentieth century

LORD, give us food for angels
and invalids, poets and madwomen,
all who find the savor of this world
too strong-mourners and saints
and those volatile souls whose joy
ignites dangerous fevers; for these
a cloud, a polished bone,
a cup of snow is sustenance enough.
Spread them a tablecloth clean

as the page of an unwritten book
and serve upon crockery
plain as a nurse: the clear broth
of memory, skim milk of exile,
cooked grains and potted
cheeses, vegetables culled
from roots of loneliness,
breast-meat, slivered
from the bony tent. Let this feast

be lean as Pharaoh's
seven dream-cows, humble to bless
the blue feet of the starving and let
each vessel, passed from hand to hand
above our plates, inscribe a circle
over circles. Let no clamorous
spice, no storm of seasoning
distract these diners
from their secret craving

to hear a mother's tongue
tolling again in the rooms
of their childhood, watch steam
rising from the early soup,
sunlight flashing from the spoon
raised like a lighthouse
over the sea, a beacon
for the hungry voyager.

Jean Nordhaus
Twentieth century

THE supper served us was a splendid one. For a friend of Mike's, Mrs. Thompson, who lives in the neighborhood and in her zeal reminds me of those early Christian women who helped spread Christianity, came in and made a feast of chile con carne, hot with peppers and, just what we needed to warm our innards, hot biscuits and large pots of coffee.

Dorothy Day
Twentieth century

TO offer hospitality to a stranger is to welcome something new, unfamiliar, and unknown into our life-world. . . . Strangers have stories to tell which we have never heard before, stories which can redirect our seeing and stimulate our imaginations. The stories invite us to view the world from a novel perspective.

Thomas Ogletree
Twentieth century

SABBATH is not only for ourselves; rested and refreshed, we more generously serve all those who need our care. The human spirit is naturally generous; the instant we are filled, our first impulse is to be useful, to be kind, to give something away. . . .

Once people feel nourished and refreshed, they cannot help but be kind; just so, the world aches for the generosity of a well-rested people.

Wayne Muller
Twentieth century

Romans 12:13

CONTRIBUTE to the needs of the saints; extend hospitality to strangers.

IN the traditions shaped by the Bible, offering hospitality is a moral imperative. The expectation that God's people are people who will welcome strangers and treat them justly runs throughout the Bible. . . .

The Hebrew Scriptures (called by many Christians the Old Testament) tell the story of the descendants of Abraham and Sarah, who answered God's call to journey far from home in search of a promised land. Later, after years of exile and slavery in Egypt, these descendants were a refugee people, wandering in a wilderness, and later still they were forced into captivity again and sent off to a distant land. As a result, their laws always required them to deal justly and compassionately with the strangers among them. . . .

Hospitality was also a crucial practice among the early Christians. One New Testament word incorporates a profound truth: *xenos,* the word that means "stranger" in Greek, also means "guest" and "host." This one word signals the essential mutuality that is at the heart of hospitality. No one is strange except in relation to someone else; we make one another guests and hosts by how we treat one another. There is a common English word that uses this same root: *xenophobia,* fear of the stranger, which is often associated with extreme nationalism or intense "my group is better than your group" attitudes. Turn this word around and make a little change, however, and you get the New Testament word for hospitality: *philoxenia,* a love of the guest or stranger. *Philoxenia* can also mean love of the whole atmosphere of hospitality and the whole activity of guesting and hosting. Indeed, within a philoxenic circle of mutuality, unexpected transformations can occur. . . .

When it is most fully realized, hospitality not only welcomes strangers; it also recognizes their holiness. It sees in the stranger a person dear to and made in the image of God, someone bearing distinctive gifts that only he or she can bring.

Ana María Pineda
Twentieth century

A classic way of carrying over the liturgy into works of mercy in the afternoon may take the form of visiting a shut-in, in a nursing home, prison, or hospital, for example. The sabbath helps slow us down to the speed of those who are in such an enforced rest, freeing us for more patience and relaxed sharing together. In such meetings we become philanthropists with time, not just with money and things. Fellowship with one's own relatives and friends also is traditional at this time. With the ever-loosening and fragmenting bonds of family and communal relationships today, the old practice of *Sunday visitin'* is not to be scorned. It helps maintain and build the social fabric of the larger community, which an inclusive sabbath peace encourages. The givenness of our relationships with family and some friends also reflects the sabbath as a given, ascribed quality of time, not an earned, achieved one.

Tilden Edwards
Twentieth century

ONE day last summer, I saw a man sitting down by one of the piers, all alone. He sat on a log, and before him was a wooden box on which he had spread out on a paper his meager supper. He sat there and ate with some pretense at human dignity, and it was one of the saddest sights I have ever seen.

Dorothy Day
Twentieth century

ONE of the customs of the sabbath is to try to make sure that no one eats meals alone. A Christian saying reminds us that a guest in the home is Christ in the home.

Peter Mazar
Twentieth century

NOW, tell me, Count" [said the young woman], "what does a guest want?"

"I believe," said Augustus when he thought for a moment, "that if we do, as I think we ought to here, leave out the crude guest, who comes to be regaled, takes what he can get and goes away, a guest wants first of all to be diverted, to get out of his daily monotony or worry. Secondly the decent guest wants to shine, to expand himself and impress his own personality upon his surroundings. And thirdly, perhaps, he wants to find some justification for this existence altogether. But since you put it so charmingly, Signora, please tell me now: What does a hostess want?"

"The hostess," said the young lady, "wants to be thanked."

Isak Dinesen
Twentieth century

WHEN we Christians rest as if all our work were done, we celebrate God's creative and redemptive accomplishments on our behalf. Knowing that God is the perfect Creator, we spend the day delighting in the beauties of his creation and thereby growing in our love for the Master Designer and Craftsman.

Observing the Sabbath gives us the opportunity to be as careful as we can to fill our lives with beauty and to share beauty with the world around us. When we observe a day especially set apart for beauty, all the rest of life is made more beautiful. . . . Focusing on beauty on one day causes us to notice it on the other six days of the week. The Sabbath becomes a garden park in the midst of the technicization of life; it brings us tranquility and intimacy, sensitivity and creativity, butterflies and goldfinches and roses!

Marva Dawn
Twentieth century

HIS left hand, in heat of noonday,
   Lovingly my head upholds,
And his right hand, filled with blessings,
   Tenderly my soul enfolds.
I adjure you, nature's darlings,
   Beautiful in field and grove,
   Stir not up, till he be willing,
Him who is my glorious Love.

Ann Griffiths
Eighteenth century

I N Exodus, Moses encounters a burning bush, and the presence of God calls out to him, "Put off your shoes from your
feet, for the place on which you are standing is holy
ground." The rabbis interpret this not so much as a warning
to Moses because this particular ground is holy, but rather
that the shoes represent something dead or foreign between
our feet and the ground on which we stand. With bare feet
Moses can literally feel the holiness come up into him, with
nothing separating his body from the tangible blessing of
sacred ground. As Brother David Steindl-Rast explains,
"Whenever we take off our shoes, we will realize that we
have been standing on holy ground."

Sabbath invites us to take off our shoes, and allow our bodies to touch the earth. Fleshy tenderness meets grass, dirt,
sand, and rock, cool and warm and sensual like a lover's
touch, feet on ground like a kiss, an embrace. Walk slowly
on a patch of ground, feel it on the feet, feel the angles,
curves, irregularities, know it the way you know the body
of a lover, every fold and mound and line.

Wayne Muller
Twentieth century

H AS anything like this ever happened to you?
You find yourself on a back country road
so beautiful to you that you ask yourself
how it could be in this world,
so impossibly lovely to you that you pull over and
tears come, as if all the griefs and sorrows
you ever felt were completing themselves, and the kingdom
you have been traveling toward all your life
were suddenly at hand, wondering what you will say
if the state trooper or the sheriff's deputy
pulls in behind you, checking to see why your car
is in a place too narrow for a car, your head
in your hands, on a strip of muddy earth
between the road, the wet ditch and the mallow,
the unharvested rice fields spread out furiously green on
        the table

flatness, the cloud mountains climbing slowly
in the feathery hot sky, the lean egrets wading
with unbroken patience and attention,
near the village of Sunset where some young girls
grow up thinking they need to be elsewhere,
see the true world, a stretch of winding road
with unphotographed houses and useful sheds,
a few brown horses grazing, and two stray dogs
leaping in and out of the roadside weeds
with the excitement of fools,
a place nowhere, and suddenly home.

Sandford Lyne
Twentieth century

W E sat down and watched [the children]. Ántonia leaned her elbows on the table. There was the deepest peace in that orchard. It was surrounded by a triple enclosure; the wire fence, then the hedge of thorny locusts, then the mulberry hedge which kept out the hot winds of summer and held fast to the protecting snows of winter. The hedges were so tall that we could see nothing but the blue sky above them, neither the barn roof nor the windmill. The afternoon sun poured down on us through the drying grape leaves. The orchard seemed full of sun, like a cup, and we could smell the ripe apples on the trees. The crabs hung on the branches as thick as beads on a string, purple-red, with a thin silvery glaze over them. Some hens and ducks had crept through the hedge and were pecking at the fallen apples. The drakes were handsome fellows, with pinkish grey bodies, their heads and necks covered with iridescent green feathers which grew close and full, changing to blue like a peacock's neck. Ántonia said they always reminded her of soldiers—some uniform she had seen in the old country, when she was a child.

Willa Cather
Twentieth century

THE grip the *present* has on me. That is the one thing
that has grown most noticeably in my spiritual life—
nothing much else has. The rest dims as it should. I am getting older. The reality of *now*—the unreality of all the rest.
The unreality of ideas and explanations and formulas. I am.
The unreality is all the rest. The pigs shriek. Butterflies dance
together—or danced together a moment ago—against the
blue sky at the end of the woodshed. The buzz saw stands
outside there, half covered with dirty and tattered canvas.
The trees are fresh and green in the sun (more rain yesterday). Small clouds inexpressibly beautiful and silent and
eloquent over the silent woodlands. What a celebration of
light, quietness, and glory! This is my feast, sitting here in
the straw!

Thomas Merton
Twentieth century

THE fume and shock and uproar
of the internal combustion of America
recede, the last vacationers gone
back to the life that drives away from home.

Bottles and wrappers of expensive
cheap feasts ride the quieted current
toward the Gulf of Mexico.

And now the breeze comes down
from the hill, the kingfisher returns
to the dead limb of the sycamore,
the swallows feed in the air
over the water.
          A muskrat draws his V
under the lowhanging willows.
In clear shallows near the rocks
tiny fish flicker and soar. A dove
sweetens the distance with his call.

Out of the frenzy of an August Sunday
the Sabbath comes. The valley glows.
A raincrow flies across the river
into the shadowy leaves. The dark falls.

Wendell Berry
Twentieth century

HOWEVER we spend the afternoon, its *drawing to a close* marks the end of the sabbath day. This closure needs special recognition, just as the sabbath's beginning does.

The Jewish community historically has developed a special ritual for ending sabbath after sundown, a rite called *havdalah,* "separation," which divides the sabbath from other days. It includes the lighting of a candle, blessings with wine and spices, quenching of the candle, and farewell songs to the sabbath.

My family has developed a closing ritual of its own that overlaps with this traditional ending, which is shared with others who happen to be with us at the time. We begin with a special supper, a kind of high tea that includes all kinds of good things to eat. We bring this food into the living room, the only time we eat there during the week. Candles are lit. A blessing is said. During the meal we talk informally about the day and sometimes about the coming week. About halfway through, one of us reads aloud to the others for about fifteen minutes. Currently this is a wondrous yet very human story about a family and its adventures. It is being read serially, week by week, until it is finished, and it is read at no other time. The story provides an ongoing drama, a window, through which we subtly see, share, and enjoy the way life can unfold in God's hidden grace and human response. It has a way of enlarging our common experience and, as well, our reference points as a family. We refer back to incidents in the story during the week as related things happen to us.

After the last bite of dessert is devoured, satisfied with this sensate sign of the yearned-for heavenly banquet, we say or sing a psalm or canticle together, give thanks for the personal presence of sabbath with us, pray for God's full shalom to come on earth, and for the ways our lives can be graced to assist and share that coming during the week.

Then we continue with the Jewish custom of passing a jar or box of spices around for everyone to smell, a reminder of the sweet savor of the sabbath to take into the week. . . . Finally we extinguish the candles with a prayer of thanksgiving for the fire of God's Spirit, which cannot be quenched.

Tilden Edwards
Twentieth century

S OMEONE *holds up the spices:*
     Our God, we thank you for the joy and rest of this day.
     As we inhale the fragrance of the spices,
     We pray that the days ahead may bring sweetness
to our lives
     and to the lives of all your children.
     May we yearn for the coming of your reign, the sabbath
without end.
     Blessed are you, Lord, God of all creation,
     Creator of the spices.
The spices are passed and all inhale their fragrance.
Then the candle is held high and one person prays:
     Blessed are you, Lord, God of all creation,
     Creator of the light of fire.
     Blessed is the Lord,
     who separated the Sabbath day from the other days.
Then the candle is extinguished. In the darkness,
the leader prays:
     The light is gone and Sabbath with it, but hope brightens
the night for us.
     Forgive our sins, O Lord, and let them be as yesterday
when it is past.
     Hear our prayer! Grant redemption!

Gabe Huck
Twentieth century

A T vanishing point:
     the color of sunset, red, intensified
then fading to the palest pink
to a mere filament of fire.
Elsewhere, the cock crows
     waking a Chinese village
     while we rock in the night's cradle
     cocooned in layers of sleep.

Thus day upon day we wait and watch:
     signs in the heavens, rain and wind

predicted storms, then a white dawn
   shivering in yards of mist.
Every day the same, the ordinary tasks:
   circle within circle, life narrowing
   into a swirling of dust.

What is left at the end?
Your light, a diamond needle
   piercing the dark at the exact point
   where everything disappears
   —breath, speech, thought—
your light waking us beyond our heartbeat
   to a surprising morning
   a continuum continually imploding into joy.

Catherine de Vinck
Twentieth century

PRESENTLY we saw a curious thing: There were no clouds, the sun was going down in a limpid, gold-washed sky. Just as the lower edge of the red disk rested on the high fields against the horizon, a great black figure suddenly appeared on the face of the sun. We sprang to our feet, straining our eyes toward it. In a moment we realized what it was. On some upland farm, a plough had been left standing in the field. The sun was sinking just behind it. Magnified across the distance by the horizontal light, it stood out against the sun, was exactly contained within the circle of the disk; the handles, the tongue, the share—black against the molten red. There it was, heroic in size, a picture writing on the sun.

Even while we whispered about it, our vision disappeared; the ball dropped and dropped until the red tip went beneath the earth. The fields below us were dark, the sky was growing pale, and that forgotten plough had sunk back to its own littleness somewhere on the prairie.

Willa Cather
Twentieth century

TRINITY of blessed light,
O Unity of princely might,
The fiery sun now goes his way;
Shed thou within our hearts thy ray.

To thee our morning song of praise,
To thee our evening prayer we raise;
Thy glory suppliant we adore
For ever and for evermore.

All laud to God the Father be,
All praise, Eternal Son, to thee,
All glory, as is ever meet,
To God the Holy Paraclete.

Saint Ambrose
Fourth century

NEVER was a victory so trumpeted,
As that of the sun climbing his fiery way
And then in gorgeous colours falling,
Trailing stars.
Life and death, water and aridity
Bow to his passing ray.

Stephen Lubega
Twentieth century

IN the beginning God created heaven,
The dark and empty earth;
His Spirit moved across the sombre waters
And stirred them with his breath.

Then God created light, and with its coming
The dark was swept away;
The morning came, and then the quiet evening:
The end of God's first day.

To God, the Father of the world give glory,
With Christ his only Son.

Who with the Spirit govern all creation:
Blest Trinity in One.

Stanbrook Abbey
Hymnal

WHILE the tomb was sealed, Christ God, life rose from the grave, and while the doors were closed, you came to the disciples, O Resurrection of all, renewing in us, through them, an upright spirit, according to the greatness of your mercy.

Orthodox liturgy

THE evening came quickly to an end. There was the humble cheerful meal, and then the bustling merry farewell, and Mary was once more in the quietness and solitude of her own dingy, dreary-looking home; her father still out, the fire extinguished, and her evening's task of work lying all undone upon the dresser. But it had been a pleasant little interlude to think upon. It had distracted her attention for a few hours from the pressure of many uneasy thoughts, of the dark, heavy, oppressive times, when sorrow and want seemed to surround her on every side.

Elizabeth Gaskell
Nineteenth century

HE who bends to himself a joy
Does the winged life destroy;
But he who kisses the joy as it flies
Lives in eternity's sunrise.

William Blake
Eighteenth century

WE resign into your hands our sleeping bodies, our cold hearths and open doors. Give us to awaken with smiles; give us to labor smiling. As the sun returns in the east, so let our patience be renewed with dawn; as the sun lightens the world, so let our loving-kindness make bright this house of our habitation.

Robert Louis
Stevenson
Nineteenth century

WE must be prepared . . . to come *away* empty-handed, with nothing left to us but a memory of delight, an increase of well-being so deep and so central and so invisibly distributed throughout the psyche that it cannot even be located, let alone measured and codified for future use.

Walter Kerr
Twentieth century

THEY walked along getting their breath, and smelling the honeysuckle in the evening. On a hill William Wallace looked down, and at the same time there went drifting by the sweet sounds of the music outdoors. They were having the Sacred Harp Sing on the grounds of an old white church glimmering there at the crossroads, far below. He stared away as if he saw it minutely, as if he could see a lady in white take a flowered cover off the organ, which was set on a little slant in the shade, dust the keys, and start to pump and play. . . . He smiled faintly, as he would at his mother, and at Hazel, and at the singing women in his life, now all one young girl standing up to sing under the trees the oldest and longest ballads there were.

Eudora Welty
Twentieth century

MUSIC ingathers all, yet takes one only
into its secret when the chimes begin.
When that great rain of sound comes down, the lonely
of spirit is elect and enters in.
Our evening shines with bells; alone, apart,
we listen, awed,
to the antiphonal pealing of our hearts.
Music by right is for the solitaries
whom a long silence trains to the profound.
The bells are ours; we come at the first airy
rumor to drench our deserts with their sound.
Yet anyone who listens may become
hermit or anchorite under that shower
when the great chimes-tree shakes its leaves of light.

Jessica Powers
Twentieth century

COLD dark deep and absolutely clear,
element bearable to no mortal,
to fish and to seals . . . One seal particularly
I have seen here evening after evening.
He was curious about me. He was interested in music;
like me a believer in total immersion,
so I used to sing him Baptist hymns.
I also sang "A Mighty Fortress Is Our God."
He stood up in the water and regarded me
steadily, moving his head a little.
Then he would disappear, then suddenly emerge
almost in the same spot, with a sort of shrug
as if it were against his better judgment.
Cold dark deep and absolutely clear,
the clear gray icy water . . . Back, behind us,
the dignified tall firs begin.
Bluish, associating with their shadows,
a million Christmas trees stand
waiting for Christmas. The water seems suspended
above the rounded gray and blue-gray stones.
I have seen it over and over, the same sea, the same,
slightly, indifferently swinging above the stones,
icily free above the stones,
above the stones and then the world.
If you should dip your hand in,
your wrist would ache immediately,
your bones would begin to ache and your hand would burn
as if the water were a transmutation of fire
that feeds on stones and burns with a dark gray flame.
If you tasted it, it would first taste bitter,
then briny, then surely burn your tongue.
It is like what we imagine knowledge to be:
dark, salt, clear, moving, utterly free,
drawn from the cold hard mouth
of the world, derived from the rocky breasts
forever, flowing and drawn, and since
our knowledge is historical, flowing, and flown.

Elizabeth Bishop
Twentieth century

As a day of prayer, communion and joy, Sunday resounds throughout society, emanating vital energies and reasons for hope. Sunday is the proclamation that time, in which he who is the Risen Lord of history makes his home, is not the grave of our illusions but the cradle of an ever new future, an opportunity given to us to turn the fleeting moments of this life into seeds of eternity. Sunday is an invitation to look ahead; it is the day on which the Christian community cries out to Christ, "*Marana tha:* Come, O Lord!" (1 Corinthians 16:22). With this cry of hope and expectation, the church is the companion and support of human hope. From Sunday to Sunday, enlightened by Christ, she goes forward toward the unending Sunday of the heavenly Jerusalem, which "has no need of the sun or moon to shine upon it, for the glory of God is its light and its lamp is the Lamb" (Revelation 21:23). . . .

Pope John Paul II
Twentieth century

Sunday will continue to shape the time of the church's pilgrimage, until that Sunday which will know no evening.

Your sun shall no more go down,
  or your moon withdraw itself;
for the LORD will be your
    everlasting light.

Isaiah 60:20ab

Lord God, whose Son our Savior Jesus Christ triumphed over the powers of death and prepared for us our place in the new Jerusalem: Grant that we, who have this day given thanks for his resurrection, may praise you in that City of which he is the light, and where he lives and reigns for ever and ever.

The Book of
Common Prayer

And thus we are brought to the last theme of Vespers: that of the *end.* It is announced by the singing of the *Nunc Dimittis.* The words are attributed in the Gospel to the old man Simeon, who had spent his life in constant expectation of the coming of the Messiah because he had been told in a vision that he would not die before he saw the promised one of Israel. When Mary and Joseph brought the child Jesus to be presented to God in the temple, he was there and received Him into his arms, and the Gospel records that he said:

> Lord, now lettest Thou Thy servant depart in peace, according to Thy word. For mine eyes have seen Thy Salvation, which Thou hast prepared before the face of all people; to be a light to lighten the Gentiles, and to be the glory of thy people Israel.

Simeon had been waiting all his life, and then at last the Christ Child was given to him: he held the Life of the world in his arms. He stood for the whole world in its expectation and longing, and the words he used to express his thanksgiving have become our own. He could recognize the Lord because he had expected Him; he took Him into his arms because it is natural to take someone you love into your arms; and then his life of waiting was fulfilled. He had beheld the One he had longed for. He had completed his purpose in life, and he was ready to die.

But death to him was no catastrophe. It was only a natural expression of the fulfillment of his waiting. He was not closing his eyes to the light he had at last seen; his death was only the beginning of a more inward vision of that light. In the same way Vespers is the recognition that the evening of this world has come which announces the day that has no evening. In this world every day faces night; the world itself is facing night. It cannot last forever. Yet the Church is affirming that an evening is not only an end, but also a beginning, just as any evening is also the beginning of another day. In Christ and through Christ it may become the beginning of a *new life,* of the day that has no evening. For our eyes have seen salvation and a light which will never fail. And because of this, the time of this world is now pregnant with new life. We come into the presence of Christ to offer Him our time, we extend our arms to receive Him. And He fills this time with Himself, He heals it and makes it— again and again—the time of salvation.

Alexander
Schmemann
Twentieth century

MEANWHILE the cross comes before the crown and tomorrow is a Monday morning. . . . It may be possible for each to think too much of his own potential glory hereafter; it is hardly possible for him to think too often or too deeply about that of his neighbour. The load, or weight, or burden of my neighbour's glory should be laid daily on my back, a load so heavy that only humility can carry it and the backs of the proud will be broken. It is a serious thing to live in a society of possible gods and goddesses, to remember that the dullest and most uninteresting person you talk to may one day be a creature which, if you saw it now, you would be strongly tempted to worship, or else a horror and a corruption such as you now meet, if at all, only in a nightmare. All day long we are, in some degree, helping each other to one or other of these destinations. It is in the light of these overwhelming possibilities, it is with the awe and the circumspection proper to them, that we should conduct all our dealings with one another, all friendships, all loves, all play, all politics. There are no *ordinary* people. You have never talked to a mere mortal. Nations, cultures, arts, civilization—these are mortal, and their life is to ours as the life of a gnat. But it is immortals whom we joke with, work with, marry, snub, and exploit—immortal horrors or everlasting splendours. This does not mean that we are to be perpetually solemn. We must play. But our merriment must be of that kind (and it is, in fact, the merriest kind) which exists between people who have, from the outset, taken each other seriously—no flippancy, no superiority, no presumption. And our charity must be a real and costly love, with deep feeling for the sins in spite of which we love the sinner—no mere tolerance or indulgence which parodies love as flippancy parodies merriment. Next to the Blessed Sacrament itself, your neighbour is the holiest object presented to your senses. If he is your Christian neighbour he is holy in almost the same way, for in him also Christ *vere latitat*—the glorifier and the glorified, Glory Himself, is truly hidden.

C. S. Lewis
Twentieth century

O LORD, my heart is not lifted up,
       my eyes are not raised too high;
I do not occupy myself with things
     too great and too marvelous for me.
But I have calmed and quieted my soul,
     like a weaned child with its mother;
     my soul is like the weaned child that is with me.

Psalm 131:1–2

THE father pours the milk from his glass
     into the cup of the child,
and as the child drinks
the whiteness, opening
her throat to the good taste
eagerly, the father is filled.
He closes the refrigerator
on its light, he walks out
under a bowl of frozen darkness
and nothing seems withheld from him.
Overhead, the burst ropes of stars,
the buckets of craters,
the chaos of heaven, absence
of refuge in the design.
Yet down here, his daughter
in her quilts, under patterns
of diamonds and novas,
full of rich milk,
sleeping.

Louise Erdrich
Twentieth century

MY soul is satisfied as with a rich feast,
   and my mouth praises you with joyful lips
when I think of you on my bed,
   and meditate on you in the watches of the night;
for you have been my help,
   and in the shadow of your wings I sing for joy.
My soul clings to you;
   your right hand upholds me.

Psalm 63:5–8

THE hare sleeps where it lies,
   With wary half-closed eyes;
The cock has ceased to crow, the hen to cluck:
Only the fox is out, some heedless duck
   Or chicken to surprise.

   Remote, each single star
   Comes out, till there they are
All shining brightly: how the dews fall damp!
While close at hand the glow-worm lights her lamp
   Or twinkles from afar.

   But evening now is done
   As much as if the sun
Day-giving had arisen in the East:
For night has come; and the great calm has ceased,
   The quiet sands have run.

Christina Rossetti
Nineteenth century

WHAT if Dante were wrong
   about paradise, the choirs
in their circular rows—what if
the celestial rose weren't petals
at all, but a commoner light,
a corona of cloves in their thin
garlic gowns, twisting up

into wicks that long to be lit,
and they are lit, flaming up
in the glory of God—
the God of the old myths
who leans over the fence
of the firmament, beyond pale
buds of new stars, leaning
our way, toward our own
common sod, sighing into it,
raising it, his breath
faintly garlic.

Margaret Gibson
Twentieth century

WHEN I look at your heavens, the work of your fingers,
the moon and the stars that you have established;
what are human beings that you are mindful of them,
mortals that you care for them?

Psalm 8:3–4

MOST holy God, the source of all good desires, all right judgments, and all just works: Give to us, your servants, that peace which the world cannot give, so that our minds may be fixed on the doing of your will, and that we, being delivered from the fear of all enemies, may live in peace and quietness; through the mercies of Christ Jesus our Savior.

*The Book of
Common Prayer*

S UNDAY is a free gift that enables us to live gracefully the rest of the week. Sunday is a day *in terms of which* we see the remaining six. It calls our attention to the future and its promise, rather than having us focus on the efforts of the past.

This notion can take on more meaning if we remember, initially, that the first day of the week is the sun's day. . . . It is the celebration of God's light coming into the world to illuminate our life: the natural light of the sun and the divine light of the Son. This means that the future, epitomized in the approaching week, is not something fearsome and dark. We enter into our life ahead with assurance, because our way is illuminated by God's presence. . . .

In setting aside the first day of the week we are then sanctifying time. The day becomes a sacrament to us, conveying by the use of that time a symbol of God's gift of light, hope, and power for the future. By accepting Sunday as holy I am able to find what enables me to live Monday through Saturday under the eternal promise of God. It is not that I now can resist the temptations of the natural world, but that I can see the daily routine as in fact the proper recipient of God's fulfilling grace.

Urban T. Holmes
Twentieth century

T HE steadfast love of the LORD never ceases,
    his mercies never come to an end;
they are new every morning;

Lamentations
3:22–23a [NRSV]

B LAZE of the Father's glory, you,
bringing your light from light's own Source.
Light from the fount of endless day,
you light the day throughout its course.

Shine down, true Sun, upon us all
with gleam that lasting light imparts,

and may the Holy Spirit, too,
bring dawn upon our waiting hearts.

Christ be for us our daily food
with faith for its initiates,
the Holy Spirit's happiness
a draught that soberly elates.

This day be joy the whole way through,
restraint its early morning light,
faith its high noon; and may the heart
escape the onset of the night.

O may the dawn forever grow,
dawn open out its total store,
Son in the Father wholly giv'n,
Father in Son for evermore.

Aelred Squire
Twentieth century

WHEN we see some of our ordinary activities as Christian practices, we come to perceive how *our daily lives are all tangled up with the things God is doing in the world.* Now we want to figure out how to pattern our practices after God's, and it becomes our deepest hope to become partners in God's reconciling love for the world. We are never able to do this perfectly, at least not for any length of time. Even so, when we set ordinary daily activities in this context, they are transformed, and so are we. A meal becomes a time of forgiveness. A day of leisure becomes a day of contemplation. An illness turns into an experience of solidarity with the poor. An occupation becomes a time of vocation. Giving becomes an expression of gratitude. A burial becomes a time of thanksgiving.

Craig Dykstra and
Dorothy C. Bass
Twentieth century

WHATEVER is foreseen in joy
Must be lived out from day to day.
Visions held open in the dark
By our ten thousand days of work.
Harvest will fill the barn; for that
The hand must ache, the face must sweat.

And yet no leaf or grain is filled
By work of ours; the field is tilled
And left to grace. That we may reap,
Great work is done while we're asleep.

When we work well, a Sabbath mood
Rests on our day, and finds it good.

Wendell Berry
Twentieth century

WHEN the tomb was shown to be open and Hades wailing, Mary cried out to the apostles who were hiding: Come out laborers of the vineyard and proclaim the news of the resurrection, for the Lord is risen, granting great mercy to the world.

Orthodox liturgy

GOD created humankind,
so that humankind might cultivate the earthly
and thereby create the heavenly.

Hildegard of Bingen
Twelfth century

IT is love of truth that looks for sanctified leisure, while it is the compulsion of love that undertakes righteous engagement in affairs.

Saint Augustine
Fifth century

TAKE pleasure in everything you do. Always be aware. Whatever we do should be just like our sacramental experiences. After all, the sacraments are there to teach us how to have daily experiences, daily bread, daily super-substantial transcendent nourishing experiences. And daily wine that rejoices our hearts. It is not only when one is before the altar that one can feel this joy. It can be experienced when we are doing whatever trivial or tedious task is the work of the moment. You've put on your alb (or apron) and taken candle (or pot) in hand, and you're going to the altar (or sink). Whatever you're doing, it is worship, it is divine expression, and it is joy. . . .

We are now the Body of Jesus in our world, in our time, in our particular locality and historical circumstances. We are the Word of God made flesh. That is the consequence of the holy communion. . . .

Jesus, being aware of himself as the Child of God in whom God is well pleased, comes to awaken us and convince us that the same is true of us. He wants to take us into his consciousness so that we can think and feel and will and see the world as he does and act in it as he does. And as fast as any of us is so transformed, catches the Jesus-consciousness, and is able to feel-think-see-will-act in that way, we are expected and empowered to pass it on, to communicate it to others: Freely you have received, freely give.

Beatrice Bruteau
Twentieth century

ABBA Poeman said concerning Abba Pior that every day he made a new beginning.

Sayings of the Desert Fathers
Fourth century

MY work is a big part of my life, but experience has taught me that other things—friends, family, time alone—fill some of my deepest needs. My youthful infatuation with myself has, happily, cooled. The inchoate "I want . . . I want" that once filled my insides, lacking any sort of clear object for that awesome verb, is muted. I want to do good work. I want to play with my children. I want to enjoy myself. I want to be happy. I once wanted to be a personage. Now I am comfortable being a person.

Anna Quindlen
Twentieth century

ALL this is God,
right here in my pea-green house
each morning
and I mean,
though often forget,
to give thanks,
to faint down by the kitchen table
in a prayer of rejoicing
as the holy birds at the kitchen window
peck into their marriage of seeds.

Anne Sexton
Twentieth century

THE Sabbath . . . cannot survive in exile, a lonely stranger among days of profanity. It needs the companionship of all other days. All days of the week must be spiritually consistent with the Day of Days. All our life should be a pilgrimage to the seventh day; the thought and appreciation of what this day may bring to us should be ever present in our minds. For the Sabbath is the counterpoint of living; the melody sustained throughout all agitations and vicissitudes which menace our conscience; our awareness of God's presence in the world.

Abraham
Joshua Heschel
Twentieth century

What *we are* depends on what *the Sabbath is* to us.

THESE coppers, big and little, these brooms and clouts and brushes, were tools; and with them one made, not shoes or cabinet-work, but life itself. One made a climate within a climate; one made the days—the complexion, the special flavour, the special happiness of each day as it passed; one made life.

Each person, as religious, stands at the center of culture. Each embodies, preserves, and furthers the human. What we do with space and time, how we live, the words we use, are of the utmost importance. Our uniqueness lies in the way that we live before God and others. Religious persons are at home in any employment. Everything is sacred. All life, each thing, every happening, holds the potential recognition of its sacredness.

The lived awareness of the presence of God in life is a gift, one given to all.

As the light grows, the service refers the new morning to the new time. As Vespers referred evening to the whole Christian experience of the world as "evening," so Matins refers morning to the Christian experience of the Church as "morning," as beginning.

These two complementary, yet absolutely essential, *dimensions* of time shape our life in time and, by giving time a new meaning, transform it into *Christian time.* This double experience is, indeed, to be applied to everything we do. We are always *between* morning and evening, *between* Sunday and Sunday, *between* Easter and Easter, *between* the two comings of Christ. The experience of time as *end* gives an absolute importance to whatever we do *now,* makes it final, decisive. The experience of time as *beginning* fills all our time with joy, for it adds to the "coefficient" of eternity: "I shall not die but live and declare the works of the Lord." We are at work in the world, and this work—in fact, any work—if analyzed in terms of the world in itself, becomes meaningless, futile, irrelevant. In every city in the world there is each morning a rush of clean and shaven people getting to work. And every evening there is a rush of the same people, now tired and dirty, going in the opposite direction. But long, long ago a wise man looked at this rush (its forms change, but not its meaninglessness) and said:

Vanity of vanities. All is vanity.
What profit hath man of all his labor which he taketh
    under the sun?
One generation passeth away and another generation
    cometh;
But the earth abideth forever.
The eye is not satisfied with seeing, nor the ear filled
    with hearing
There is no new thing under the sun. . . . (Ecclesiates 1)

And this remains true of the *fallen* world. But we Christians have too often forgotten that God has redeemed the world. For centuries we have preached to the hurrying people: your daily rush has no meaning, yet accept it—and you will be rewarded in *another* world by an eternal rest. But God revealed and offers us eternal Life and not eternal rest. And God revealed this eternal Life in the midst of time—and of its *rush*—as its secret meaning and goal. And thus he made time, and our work in it, into the *sacrament of the world to come,* the liturgy of fulfillment and ascension. It is when we have reached the very end of the world's self-sufficiency that it *begins* again for us as the material of the sacrament that we are to fulfill in Christ.

"There is no new thing under the sun." Yet every day, every minute resounds now with the victorious affirmation: "Behold, I make all things new. I am Alpha and Omega, the beginning and the end . . ." (Revelation 21:5–6).

Alexander
Schmemann
Twentieth century

THE late poet Paul Zweig once wrote, "If there is an Eden, it is not past, but coming," and this gives me the confidence to say that . . . we might best confront the mystery of our daily lives by doing as Jesus suggests, and look to small children, who have a wondrous capacity for living in the present moment with an innocent hope in what they learn to call the future. When my niece Christina was a toddler—she is now twenty—her mother worked as a stockbroker and financial planner. My brother, Christina's father, who is a Disciples of Christ pastor, would drive her to day care in the morning, and her mother would pick her up after work. And every afternoon she brought Christina an orange, peeled so that the child could eat it on the way home. One day Christina was busying herself by playing "Mommy's office" on the front porch of our house in Honolulu, and I asked her what her mother did at work. Without hesitation, and with a conviction that I relish to this day, she looked up at me and said, "She makes oranges."

Kathleen Norris
Twentieth century

REJOICE always, pray without ceasing, give thanks in all circumstances; for this is the will of God in Christ Jesus for you.

1 Thessalonians
5:16–18

Endnotes

Unless otherwise indicated, scripture quotations are from the *New Revised Standard Version* of the Bible, copyright © 1989 by the Division of Christian Education of the National Council of the Churches of Christ in the USA. Used by permission. All rights reserved.

Excerpts from the English translation of the Roman Missal, © 1973 ICEL.

Excerpts from Pope John Paul II's Apostolic Letter **Dies Domini** are from *A Guide to Keeping Sunday Holy,* Copyright © 1988 Archdiocese of Chicago: Liturgy Training Publications.

Excerpts from *At That Time: Cycles and Seasons in the Life of a Christian* edited by James A. Wilde, © 1989 Archdiocese of Chicago: Liturgy Training Publications.

Excerpts from *The Liturgical Year* translated by Matthew J. O'Connell, Pueblo Publishing Company, 1981.

Excerpts from *The Sabbath: Its Meaning for Modern Man* by Abraham Joshua Heschel. Copyright © 1951 by Abraham Joshua Heschel. Copyright renewed 1979 by Sylvia Heschel.

Introduction

"Without Sunday: Quoted by Pope John Paul II in *Dies Domini,* 46.

Prelude

(1) **Soon enough:** From *Sabbath* by Wayne Muller, copyright © 1999 by Wayne Muller. Used by permission of Bantam Books, a division of Random House, Inc.

The resurrection of Jesus: *Dies Domini.*

At the source of our celebrations: *The Wellspring of Worship* translated by Matthew J. O'Connell, Paulist Press, 1988.

Sabbath after Sabbath: From "The Christian Week" by Peter Mazar in *At That Time.*

The origin of the seven-day week: "A response to R. Goldenberg and D. J. Harrington, SJ," in *The*

Sabbath in Jewish and Christian Traditions, 1991. Reprinted with permission of the University of Denver.

The way in which time: in *Practicing Our Faith* edited by Dorothy C. Bass, copyright © 1997 by Jossey-Bass, Inc., Publishers. This material is used by permission of John Wiley & Sons, Inc.

The actual origins: *Seasons and Feasts of the Year* by Michael D. Whalen, Paulist Press, Inc., www.paulistpress.com.

Modernity has had: From "The Sanctoral Cycle" by Lawrence S. Cunningham in *At That Time.*

The word feria: *Catholic Ceremonies,* Benziger Brothers, 1896.

The sabbath plays: *The Liturgical Year.*

Nehemiah relates: Reprinted from *Sabbath, the Day of Delight,* © 1965, by Abraham Millgram, published by The Jewish Publication Society with the permission of the publisher, The Jewish Publication Society.

The Christian celebration: From *The Church at Prayer,* Volume IV of *The Liturgy and Time* translated by Matthew J. O'Connell, published by The Liturgical Press, copyright © 1986 by The Order of St. Benedict, Inc., Collegeville, Minnesota. All rights reserved.

In Abitina: *Butler's Lives of the Saints,* Burns & Oates, a Continuum imprint. Reproduced with permission of the Continuum International Publishing Group Ltd.

It was Jerome:"Sunday—Being Made Whole in the Company of Others" in *Liturgy* 20 (April 1975), © 1975 The Liturgical Conference, Inc. All rights reserved. Used by permission.

While "servile work": "Catholic Sunday in America" in *Sunday Morning: A Time for Worship* edited by Mark Searle, published by The Liturgical Press, 1982. Used with permission of the Notre Dame Center for Liturgy.

The first redaction: *The Liturgical Year.*   (10)

The Sabbath precept: *Dies Domini.*

The third commandment: "Holy Leisure and the Sabbath Tradition" in *Liturgy* 8 (1987), © 1987 The Liturgical Conference, Inc. All rights reserved. Used by permission.

The Sabbath commandment: *Practicing Our Faith* edited by Dorothy C. Bass, copyright © 1997 by Jossey-Bass, Inc., Publishers. This material is used by permission of John Wiley & Sons, Inc.

All concepts of melakhah: Reprinted from *The Jewish Catalog: A Do-It-Yourself Kit,* © 1973, by

Richard Siegel, Michael Strassfeld and Sharon Strassfeld, published by The Jewish Publication Society with the permission of the publisher, The Jewish Publication Society.

One of the: *The Sabbath: Its Meaning for Modern Man.*

In our biblical: "Sunday: the Day that is Different" in *Major Feasts and Seasons,* 2 (1977), © 1977 The Liturgical Conference, Inc. All rights reserved. Used by permission.

What is meant: *Sabbath Time* by Tilden Edwards, The Seabury Press, 1982.

To be sure: "The Place of the Sabbath in Rabbinic Judaism" in *The Sabbath in Jewish and Christian Traditions,* 1991. Reprinted with permission of the University of Denver.

God made: *Come to Think of It . . . ,* Dodd, Mead & Company, 1931. Used with permission.

Where I come from: Nigerian drummer, *Simply Living, the Spirit of the Indigenous People* edited by Shirley Ann Jones. New World Library, 1999. Used with permission.

We have familiar: *Sermons Preached on Various Occasions,* Longmans, Green, and Company, 1898.

We can: From *Sabbath* by Wayne Muller, copyright © 1999 by Wayne Muller. Used by permission of Bantam Books, a division of Random House, Inc.

Our calendars: *The Way of the Heart* by Henry Nouwen, The Seabury Press, 1981.

How many: Poems from *The Timbered Choir, Sabbath Poems 1979–1997,* copyright 1998 by Wendell Berry. Reprinted by permission of his publisher. All rights reserved.

In a contrary: From *The Decline of Pleasure* by Walter Kerr, Simon and Schuster, 1962. Used by permission of Christopher Kerr.

(20) **My father:** "It Takes More Than Elbow Grease to Build a Full Life," copyright September 3, 2000, *Chicago Tribune.*

We eat: Reprinted with permission. Taken from *Sabbath Bread* by Georgene L. Wilson, © 1987, published by Resource Publications, Inc., www.resourcepublications.com.

Life goes wrong: *The Sabbath: Its Meaning for Modern Man.*

I can't understand: Ladakhi villager, *Simply Living, the Spirit of the Indigenous People* edited by Shirley Ann Jones. New World Library, 1999. Used with permission.

It isn't only: Copyright © 2000 From *My Job My Self* by Al Gini. Reproduced by permission of Routledge/Taylor & Francis Books, Inc.

If the inhabitants: "Jewish Observance, Sabbath and Family Life" in *Liturgy* 20 (1975) © 1975 The Liturgical Conference, Inc. All rights reserved. Used by permission.

A saying: from *Messengers of God* by Elie Wiesel. Copyright © 1976 by Elie Wiesel. Reprinted by permission of Georges Borchardt, Inc. for the author.

Time: Reprinted with the permission of Simon & Schuster Adult Publishing Group, from *How to Run a Traditional Jewish Household* by Blu Goldberg. Copyright © 1983 by Blu Greenberg. All rights reserved.

Can we: in *Major Feasts and Seasons* 2 (1977), © 1977 The Liturgical Conference, Inc. All rights reserved. Used by permission.

Once, when: *Violence Unveiled.* Crossroad Publishing Company, 1995.

Friday

The light: From "A Wall of Fire Rising" in *Krik? Krak!* by Edwidge Danticat (Soho Press, NY; Vintage, NY).

My mother: From *Diaries of Mario M. Cuomo* by Mario M. Cuomo, copyright © 1984 by Mario M. Cuomo. Used by permission of Random House, Inc.

God, bless: *God of a Hundred Names* collected and arranged by Barbara Greene and Victor Gollancz, Doubleday & Company, 1963.

When I think: Excerpt from *The Quotidian Mysteries* by Kathleen Norris. Copyright © 1998 by Kathleen Norris. Paulist Press, Inc, New York/Mahwah, NJ. Used with permission of Paulist Press, www.paulistpress.com.

Friday in Lemoa: Used with permission of Sr. Regina Bechtle, SC, Sisters of Charity of New York.

"Father,": From *Shadows on the Rock* by Willa Cather, copyright 1931 by Willa Cather and renewed 1959 by the Executors of the Estate of Willa Cather. Used by permission of Alfred A. Knopf, a division of Random House, Inc.

It is about: From *Working.* Reprinted by permission of Donadio & Olson, Inc. Copyright 1972 by Studs Terkel.

(29) **I have just:** From *Squandering Aimlissly, My Adventures in the American Marketplace* by David Brancaccio. Copyright © 2000 by David Brancaccio. Abridged by permission of Simon & Schuster Adult Publishing Group.

A desperate: *One Sunset a Week.* E. P. Dutton & Co., Inc., copyright © 1974 by George Vecsey. George Vecsey, a sports columnist, has covered both religion and the Appalachian region for the *New York Times,* and wrote *One Sunset a Week* in 1974 with the cooperation of a coal-mining family in southwest Virginia. Used by permission of the author.

You eatin': *My Friend's Got This Problem, Mr. Candler,* Clarion Books, copyright © 1991 by Mel Glenn. The author is a teacher, writer living in Brooklyn, NY. His website is www.melglenn.com.

They mow: Excerpt from pages 2 and 3 from *microserfs,* by Douglas Coupland.Copyright © 1995 by Douglas Coupland. Reprinted by permission of HarperCollins Publishers, Inc.

Our life: "God in the Kitchen" in *Spirituality and the Jewish-Christian Dialogue.* Reproduced by permission of The Way, Campion Hall, Oxford OX1 1QS.

Robert Bridges: Excerpt from Letter "To William Sessions 8 July 56" from *The Habit of Being: Letters of Flannery O'Connor* edited by Sally Fitzgerald. Copyright © 1979 by Regina O'Connor.

Come then: in *Roots, Deep and Strong, Great Men and Women of the Church* by Mary E. Penrose, OSB, Paulist Press, www.paulistpress.com.

There is none: "Editorial," by Dorothy Day in *The Catholic Worker,* October 1934. Used with permission.

Oysters and: *Much Depends on Dinner,* Macmillan Publishing Company, copyright © 1986 by Margaret Visser.

One reason: from "The Christian Week" by Peter Mazar in *At That Time.*

We come: in *The Communion of Saints, Prayers of the Famous,* edited by Horton Davies, William B. Eerdmans Publishing Company, 1990.

All night: "Easter Night" by Alice Meynell in *A Book of Religious Verse* edited by Helen Gardner, Oxford University Press, 1972.

Christ our Savior: Hymn from Byzantine Saturday Vespers, Tone II translated by J. Michael Thompson.

My love: "Wardrobe" by M. Madaleva, CSC, from *Collected Poems,* 1947. Used with permission of the Congregation of the Sisters of the Holy Cross.

When the wood: *Liturgy and Social Justice* edited by Mark Searle, published by The Liturgical Press, 1980. Used with permission of the Notre Dame Center for Liturgy.

Thousands of geese: From "Again this Winter" in *Blessings the Body Gave* by Walt McDonald. Ohio State University Press, copyright © 1998 by Walter McDonald. Used by permission of the author.

One evening: From *Living Out Loud* by Anna Quindlen, copyright © 1987 by Anna Quindlen. Used by permission of Random House, Inc. For the United Kingdom and British Commonwealth: Reprinted by permission of International Creative Management, Inc. Copyright © 1987.

She said: "The 5:32," copyright 1941 by Phyllis McGinley from *Times Three* by Phyllis McGinley, copyright 1932–1960 by Phyllis McGinley; copyright 1938–42, 1944, 1945, 1958, 1959 by The Curtis Publishing Co. Used by permission of Viking Penguin, a division of Penguin Group (USA) Inc.

I leant: "The Darkling Thrush" by Thomas Hardy. Reprinted with the permission of Scribner, an imprint of Simon & Schuster Adult Publishing Group, from *The Complete Poems of Thomas Hardy* by James Gibson. Copyright © 1925 by The Macmillan Company.

When icicles: From *Love's Labour's Lost* in *The Works of Shakespeare* edited by H. C. Hart, Methuen and Co. Ltd., 1930. Used by permission of Thompson Publishing Services.

On the sixth: Copyright © 1994 Camaldolese Hermits of America. Used with permission.

With shadows: In *Hymns for Morning and Evening Prayer,* Liturgy Training Publications; hymn texts © 1999 Aelred-Seton Shanley.

Shabbat

A friend: Reprinted with the permission of Simon & Schuster Adult Publishing Group, from *How to Run a Traditional Jewish Household* by Blu Goldberg. Copyright © 1983 by Blu Greenberg. All rights reserved.

Even the poorest: *Code of Jewish Law* by Rabbi Solomon Ganzfried, translated by Hyman E. Goldin, © copyright 1961, 1963 by Hebrew Publishing Company, New York.

And so: *The Joys of Yiddish,* by Leo Rosten, McGraw Hill, copyright © 1968 by Leo Rosten. Used with permission.

At the: From *Holy Days: the World of a Hasidic Family* by Lis Harris. Copyright © 1985 by Lis Harris. Abridged by permission of Simon & Schuster Adult Publishing Group.

Come, my and **When the world:** *Gates of Shabbat, a Guide for Observing Shabbat* by Mark Dov Shapiro, copyright © 1991 Central Conference of American Rabbis, NY.

The idea: *The Sabbath, Its Meaning for Modern Man.*

Traditional Judaism: Reprinted with the permission of Simon & Schuster Adult Publishing Group, from *How to Run a Traditional Jewish Household* by Blu Goldberg. Copyright © 1983 by Blu Greenberg. All rights reserved.

The sweet: "Wellfleet Shabbat" from *The Art of Blessing the Day* by Marge Piercy, copyright © 1999 by Middlemarsh, Inc. Used by permission of Alfred A. Knopf, a division of Random House, Inc.

She quickly: *Burning Lights,* Copyright 1946 by Schocken Books, Inc.

(50) **Psalm 92:** From *To Pray As a Jew* by Rabbi Hayim Halevy Donin. Copyright © 1980 by Rabbi Hayim Halevy Donin. Reprinted by permission of Basic Books, a member of Perseus Books, LLC.

We were: from *The Landsmen* by Peter Martin, Southern Illinois University Press, copyright 1952 by Peter Martin.

Come, O: *Gates of Prayer,* copyright © 1975 Central Conference of American Rabbis, NY.

In the most: *The Spirit of the Ghetto,* copyright 1902, 1965 by Funk & Wagnalls Company, Inc.

They say: "Sabbath Eve" was first published in 1996 in *The Other Side of the Hill, 1975—1995,* Forest Woods Media Productions, Inc.

Sabbath brings: Reprinted from *Life Is with People* by Mark Zborowski. By permission of International Universities Press, Inc. Copyright © 1952 by International Universities Press, Inc.

Judaism is: *The Sabbath, Its Meaning for Modern Man.*

I leave it: *The Joys of Yiddish,* by Leo Rosten, McGraw Hill, copyright © 1968 by Leo Rosten. Used with permission.

My friend: From *Sabbath* by Wayne Muller, copyright © 1999 by Wayne Muller. Used by permission of Bantam Books, a division of Random House, Inc.

In the home: "The Place of the Sabbath in Rabbinic Judaism" in *The Sabbath in Jewish and Christian Traditions,* 1991. Reprinted with permission of the University of Denver.

Approaching the: From *Davita's Harp* by Chaim Potok, copyright © 1985 by Chaim Potok. Used by permission of Alfred A. Knopf, a division of Random House, Inc.

A pious Jew: From *My Mother's Sabbath Days* by Chaim Grade, translated by Channa Goldstein, copyright © 1986 by the Estate of Chaim Grade. Used by permission of Alfred A. Knopf, a division of Random House, Inc.

A rite of: "Jewish Observance, Sabbath and Family Life" in *Liturgy* 20 (1975) © 1975 The Liturgical Conference, Inc. All rights reserved. Used by permission.

The third meal: "The Place of the Sabbath in Rabbinic Judaism" in *The Sabbath in Jewish and Christian Traditions,* 1991. Reprinted with permission of the University of Denver.

We give: *Gates of the House,* copyright © 1976, Central Conference of American Rabbis, NY.

Shabbat is: Reprinted with the permission of Simon & Schuster Adult Publishing Group, from *How to Run a Traditional Jewish Household* by Blu Goldberg. Copyright © 1983 by Blu Greenberg. All rights reserved.

We praise: *Gates of Prayer,* copyright © 1994, Central Conference of American Rabbis. All rights reserved.

Saturday

Once again: *The Reed of God* by Caryll Houselander. New York: Sheed & Ward, 1954, copyright 1944, by Sheed & Ward, Inc. Sheed & Ward is an imprint of the Rowman & Littlefield Publishing Group.

If the Church: *Catholic Ceremonies,* Benziger Brothers, 1896.

As depicted: "Mary of Nazareth: Friend of God and Prophet," *America* 182 (June 17–24, 2000), copyright 2000. All rights reserved. Excerpts reprinted with permission of America Press. For subscription information, visit www.americamagazine.org.

Therefore the: Excerpt from scripture is from the (60) *New American Bible with Revised New Testament and Psalms,* Copyright © 1991, 1986, 1970 Confraterniy of Christian Doctrine, Inc., Washington, DC. Used with permission. All rights reserved. No portion of the *New American Bible* may be reprinted without permission in writing from the copyright holder.

With the: Excerpt from chapter 13 of JULIAN OF NORWICH: *Showings,* from The Classics of Western Spirituality, translated from the critical text with an introduction by Edmund Colledge, OSA, and James Walsh, SJ. Copyright © 1978 by Paulist Press, Inc., New York/Mahwah, NJ. Used with permission of Paulist Press, www.paulistpress.com.

With Mary: *Dies Domini.*

At the message: from *The Documents of Vatican II,* Walter M. Abbott, SJ, General Editor; copyright 1966 by America Press. Reprinted with permission.

If it's: From *The Chicago Tribune Magazine,* copyright September 25, 1988, *Chicago Tribune.*

Weekends in: "It Takes More Than Elbow Grease to Build a Full Life," copyright September 3, 2000, *Chicago Tribune.*

Johnny, the: "What the Living Do," from *What the Living Do* by Marie Howe. Copyright © 1997 by Marie Howe. Used by permission of W. W. Norton & Company, Inc.

My father: from "Work" by Gregory Fraser in *The Southern Review* 36 (Winter 2000). Gregory Fraser's first collection of poems, *Strange Pietà,* was published in 2003 by Texas Tech University Press.

Margaret's garden: from "A Million Dollar Story" in *A Week in South Dakota, Stories* by Gary Gildner. © 1987 by Gary Gildner. Reprinted by permission of Algonquin Books of Chapel Hill.

After hours: Reprinted by permission of Louisiana State University Press from *Signs: Poems* by Margaret Gibson. Copyright © 1979 by Margaret Gibson.

It was afternoon: Excerpt from "The Wide Net" from *The Wide Net and Other Stories,* copyright 1942 and renewed 1970 by Eudora Welty, reprinted by permission of Harcourt, Inc.

It was Saturday: from "The Sharing of Bread" from *The Foreign Legion, Stories and Chronicles* by Clarice Lispector, translated by Giovanni Pontiero, Carcanet Press, 1986, copyright © Giovanni Pontiero, 1986. Used by Permission of Carcanet Press.

First of all: From *Around the Year with the Trapp Family,* Pantheon, 1955. Used by permission of Jane Weaver, President, Trapp Family Lodge, Inc.

(68) **Remembering:** Excerpts from *Catholic Household Blessings and Prayers* Copyright © 1988, United States Conference of Catholic Bishops, Washington, DC. Used with permission. All rights reserved. No part of this work may be reproduced or transmitted in any form without the permission in writing from the copyright holder.

How do: "Sunday: the Day That Is Different" in *Major Feasts and Seasons 2* (1977) © 1977 The Liturgical Conference, Inc. All rights reserved. Used by permission.

Across the: "The Swan" from *House of Light* by Mary Oliver. Copyright © 1990 by Mary Oliver. Reprinted by permission of Beacon Press, Boston.

When you: Excerpt from *The Long Loneliness* by Dorothy Day. Illustrated by Fritz Elchenberg. Copyright 1952 by Harper & Row, Publishers, Inc.; renewed © 1980 by Tamar Teresa Hennessy. Reprinted by permission of HarperCollins Publishers Inc.

A scarf: "Shabbat Moment" from *The Art of Blessing the Day* by Marge Piercy, copyright © 1999 by Middlemarsh, Inc. Used by permission of Alfred A. Knopf, a division of Random House, Inc.

Whosoever would: From *Celtic Invocations,* selections from Volume I of *Carmina gadelica* by Alexander Carmichael, Vineyard Books, 1977.

The old: From *Sabbath* by Wayne Muller, copyright © 1999 by Wayne Muller. Used by permission of Bantam Books, a division of Random House, Inc.

Don't surrender: "Don't surrender your loneliness" from *The Subject Tonight Is Love: 60 Wild and Sweet Poems of Hafiz,* translated by Daniel Ladinsky. Copyright © 1996 by Pumpkin House Press. Hafiz is a fourteenth-century Persian poet.

God in: From *The Prayers of Kierkegaard,* edited by Perry D. LeFevre, University of Chicago Press, 1956. Used by permission of the University of Chicago Press.

O God: *Prayers for Pastor and People* compiled and edited by Carl G. Carlozzi. Church Publishing, 1984.

All of us: Hymn from Byzantine Saturday Vespers, Tone III, translated by J. Michael Thompson.

On Saturday: From *Springtime of the Liturgy* by Lucien Deiss, translated by Matthew J. O'Connell, published by The Liturgical Press, © 1979 by The Order of St. Benedict, Inc. Used with permission.

We offer: Hymn from Byzantine Saturday Vespers, Tone III, translated by J. Michael Thompson.

I try: From "For God in My Sorrows" in *Blessings the Body Gave* by Walt McDonald. Ohio State Unversity Press, copyright ©1998 by Walter McDonald. Used by permission of the author.

O Brightness Hymn text translated from second–third century Greek by E. W. Eddis, 1864.

O most: "Night of Storm" from *Selected Poetry of Jessica Powers* edited by Regina Siegfried, ASC, and Robert F. Morneau, ICS Publications, Washington, DC. All copyrights, Carmelite Monastery, Pewaukee, Wisconsin. Used with permission.

Someone has: "Fishing on a Lake at Night" from *This Tree Will Be Here for a Thousand Years,* Revised Edition by Robert Bly. Copyright © 1979, 1992 by Robert Bly. Reprinted by permission of HarperCollins Publishers Inc.

Jesus whom: Translated by Gerard Manley Hopkins in *The Communion of Saints, Prayers of the Famous,* edited by Horton Davies, William B. Eerdmans Publishing Company, 1990.

Apart from: From *The Church at Prayer,* Volume IV of *The Liturgy and Time* translated by Matthew J. O'Connell, published by The Liturgical Press, copyright © 1986 by The Order of St. Benedict, Inc., Collegeville, Minnesota. All rights reserved. Used with permission.

When servants: From *The Syriac Fathers on Prayer and the Spiritual Life,* translated and edited by Sebastian Brock, Cistercian Fathers Studies: Number 101. Copyright Cistercian Publications, Kalamazoo, MI, 1987.

If, preparing: From *The Sayings of the Desert Fathers,* translated by Benedicta Ward, SLG, Cistercian Fathers Series: Number 59. Published by Cistercian Publications, Kalamazoo, MI, 1975.

One of: From "The Christian Day" by Andrew D. Ciferni in *At That Time.*

(78) **It was:** From *Patrologia Graeca* XXV, 673–6 translated in *Music in Early Christian Literature* edited by James McKinnon, © Cambridge University Press, 1987. Reprinted with the permission of Cambridge University Press.

These were: "Dancing with My Sisters" in *Ordinary Mysteries, More Chronicles of Life, Love and Laughter* © 1991 by Stephen J. Vicchio, Wakefield Editions, 1991.

Tim: Extract from *Nuns and Soldiers* by Iris Murdoch published by Chatto & Windus. Used by permission of The Random House Group Limited.

Margaret likes: From "A Million-Dollar Story" in *A Week in South Dakota, Stories* by Gary Gildner. © 1987 by Gary Gildner. Reprinted by permission of Algonquin Books of Chapel Hill.

I could: "Juke Box Love Song" from *The Collected Poems of Langston Hughes* by Langston Hughes, copyright © 1994 by the Estate of Langston Hughes. Used by permission of Alfred A. Knopf, a division of Random House, Inc. For United Kingdom: Reprinted by permission of Harold Ober Associates Incorporated.

Sunday Early Morning

Sundays too: "Those Winter Sundays" From *Angle of Ascent: New and Selected Poems by Robert Hayden* Liveright Publishing Corporation, copyright © 1975 by Robert Hayden.

This is: From *The Mennonite Hymnal.* © 1969 Herald Press: Scottdale, PA 15693. Used by permission.

It is a: "Country Club Sunday" From *Times Three* by Phyllis McGinley, copyright 1932–1960 by Phyllis McGinley; copyright 1938–42, 1944, 1945, 1958, 1959 by The Curtis Publishing Co. Used by permission of Viking Penguin, a division of Penguin Group (USA) Inc.

John Vianney: From "Sunday—Being Made Whole in the Company of Others" in *Liturgy* 20 (April 1975), © 1975 The Liturgical Conference, Inc. All rights reserved. Used by permission.

From the: From "Doing the Rights Thing," interview with Kweisi Mfume by Claudia Dreifus in *Modern Maturity* (March–April 2000). © Copyright Claudia Dreyfus. Used with permission.

Complacencies: From "Sunday Morning" in *The Collected Poems of Wallace Stevens* by Wallace Stevens, copyright 1954 by Wallace Stevens and renewed 1982 by Holly Stevens. Used by permission of Alfred Al Knopf, a division of Random House, Inc.

You rose: In *The Service of the Sunday Orthros* translated by N. Michael Vaporis. Reprinted by permission of Holy Cross Orthodox Press.

O come: Text: Thomas H. Troeger (born 1945) from *Borrowed Light* © 1994 Oxford University Press, Inc. Used by permission. All rights reserved. Photocopying this copyright material is *illegal.*

Over the: "Let There Be Light" From *Selected Poetry of Jessica Powers* edited by Regina Siegfried, ASC, and Robert F. Morneau published by ICS Publications, Washington, DC. All copyrights, Carmelite Monastery, Pewaukee WI. Used with permission.

Transcendent God: in *The Stanbrook Abbey Hymnal* © Stanbrook Abbey 1974. Used with permission.

Sunday morning: Excerpt from *Dakota* by Kathleen Norris. Copyright © 1993 by Kathleen Norris. Reprinted by permission of Houghton Mifflin Company. All rights reserved.

This is: "This Is A Day of New Beginnings." Words: Brian Wren. © 1983, rev. 1987 Hope Publishing Company, Carol Stream, IL 60188. All rights reserved. Used by permission.

When you: in *The Service of the Sunday Orthros* translated by N. Michael Vaporis. Reprinted by permission of Holy Cross Orthodox Press.

How does: "Alone at Dawn with the Blinds Raised" by Walt McDonald in *All Occasions* by Walt McDonald, University of Notre Dame Press, 2000. Used by permission of the author.

When Mama: From *Papa's Wife* by Thyra Ferré Bjorn. Copyright © 1955 by Thyra Ferré Bjorn. Copyright renewed 1983 by Robert J. Bjorn. Reprinted by permission of Henry Holt and Company, LLC.

Christianity: In *Selections from Ralph Waldo Emerson, An Organic Anthology* edited by Stephen E. Whicher. Houghton Mifflin Company, 1957.

Then she: From *Mary Barton, A Tale of Manchester Life* by Elizabeth Gaskell, Penguin Books, 1970.

Blessed be: Deacon's proclamation in honor of the Lord's Day from the Syriac text in the *Missal of the Church of Antioch of the Maronites* (edition in Syriac and Arabic), Jounich (Lebanon) 1959, p. 38 quoted in *Dies Domini.*

Oh, the: From *Diaries of Mario M. Cuomo* by Mario M. Cuomo, copyright © 1984 by Mario M. Cuomo. Used by permission of Random House, Inc.

After a: From *Sabbath Time* by Tilden Edwards, The Seabury Press, 1982.

In houses: From *Gather Faithfully Together, Guide for Sunday Mass,* Archdiocese of Chicago: Liturgy Training Publications, 1997.

We pray: In *Springtime of the Liturgy, Liturgical Texts of the First Four Centuries* by Lucien Deiss, translated by Matthew J. O'Connell, The Liturgical Press, Copyright © 1979 by The Order of St. Benedict, Inc., Collegeville, Minnesota. Used with permission.

Some keep: Reprinted by permission of the publishers and the Trustees of Amherst College from *The Poems of Emily Dickinson,* Thomas H. Johnson, ed., Cambridge Mass.: The Belknap Press of Harvard University Press, Copyright © 1951, 1955, 1979 by the President and Fellows of Harvard College.

Sunday Morning Liturgy

When you: In *Springtime of the Liturgy, Liturgical Texts of the First Four Centuries* by Lucien Deiss, translated by Matthew J. O'Connell, The Liturgical Press, Copyright © 1979 by The Order of St. Benedict, Inc., Collegeville, Minnesota. Used with permission.

Most glorious: From *Poetical Works,* edited by J. C. Smith and E. de Selincourt, 1 volume, Oxford University Press, London, 1912.

In every: From *The Catholic Thing* published by Templegate Publishers, Springfield, Illinois, copyright © 1979 by Rosemary Haughton. Used with permission.

Most of: From *Traveling Mercies* by Anne Lamott, copyright © 1999 by Anne Lamott. Used by permission of Pantheon Books, a division of Random House, Inc.

There is: Excerpt from pages 57–59 from *Holy the Firm* by Annie Dillard. Copyright © 1977 by Annie Dillard. Reprinted by permission of HarperCollins Publishers Inc.

About Sunday: From *Reviving Sacred Speech: The Meaning of Liturgical Language* © The Order of Saint Luke (Akron, OH: OSL Publications). Used by permission.

Great grandmother "Praise" by Chris Llewellyn in *The Other Side of the Hill, 1975–1995,* Forest Woods Media Productions Inc., Washington, DC. Chris Llewellyn is an instructor in creative writing at the Writer's Center in Bethseda, MD. Her book of poems, *Fragments from the Fire, the Triangle Shirtwaise Company Fire of March 25, 1911,* won the Walt Whitman Award from the Academy of American Poets and she has received the Fellowship in Literature Grant from the National Endowment for the Arts.

Safely through: In *The Covenant Hymnal, Covenant Press,* Chicago.

Those who: From *Dies Domini.*

On the: From *Gather Faithfully Together, Guide for Sunday Mass,* Archdiocese of Chicago: Liturgy Training Publications, 1997.

This principle: From *The Meaning of Sunday* by J. A. Jungmann, SJ, translated by Clifford Howell, SJ, published by Fides Publishers, Notre Dame, IN, © 1961 by Challoner Publications (Liturgy) Ltd.

With a: From "The Ones Who Walk Away from Omelas" in *The Wind's Twelve Quarters.* Copyright © 1973, 1975 by Ursula K. Le Guin.

The venerable: Excerpts from MAXIMUS CONFESSOR: *Selected Writings,* translation and notes by George C. Berthold, from *The Classics of Western Spirituality,* copyright © 1985 by George Berthold, Paulist Press, Inc., New York/Mahwah, NJ. Used with permission of Paulist Press, www.paulistpress.com.

Come Sunday: "Come Sunday" from *Come Sunday* written by Nikki Grimes; Illustrated by Michael Bryant. Copyright 1996. Published by Eerdmans Publishing Company. (800) 253-7521, www.eerdmans.com/youngreaders. Used by permission, all rights reserved.

The door: From *Fair Annie of Old Mule Hollow* published by Avon Publishers, copyright © 1978 by Beverly Courtney Crook.

In those: In *A Rocking-Horse Catholic* by Caryll Houselander. New York: Sheed & Ward, copyright 1955 by Sheed and Ward, Inc. Sheed & Ward is an imprint of the Rowman & Littlefield Publishing Group.

Come you: From *Byzantine Daily Worship,* Copyright: Alleluia Press, Allendale, NJ 07401, 1995.

On the: In *Springtime of the Liturgy, Liturgical Texts of the First Four Centuries* by Lucien Deiss, translated by Matthew J. O'Connell, The Liturgical Press, copyright © 1979 by The Order of St. Benedict, Inc., Collegeville, Minnesota. Used with permission.

Lord, shall: Excerpt from "Choruses from the Rock" in *Collected Poems 1909–1962* by T. S. Eliot copyright 1936 by Harcourt, Inc., copyright © 1964, 1963 by T. S. Eliot, reprinted by permission of the publisher.

The Day: In *The Faith of the Early Fathers,* Volume One, selected and translated by W. A. Jurgens, © 1970 The Liturgical Press, Collegeville, Minnesota. Used with permission.

All people: "Psalm 100" by William Kethe in *The New Oxford Book of Christian Verse* chosen and edited by Donald Davie, Oxford University Press, 1981. Used with permission.

It is important: From *Dies Domini.*

It is not surprising: From "Singing Our Lives" by Don E. Saliers in *Practicing Our Faith* edited by Dorothy C. Bass, copyright © 1997 by Jossey-Bass Publishers.

It is not you: Excerpt from page 61 from *Life Together* by Dietrich Bonhoeffer and translated by John Doberstein. English translation copyright © 1954 by Harper & Brothers, copyright renewed 1982 by Helen S. Doberstein. Reprinted by permission of HarperCollins Publications Inc.

Tambourines!: From *The Collected Poems of Langston Hughes* by Langston Hughes, copyright © 1994 by the Estate of Langston Hughes. Used by permission of Alfred A. Knopf, a division of Random House, Inc. For United Kingdom: Reprinted by permission of Harold Ober Associates Incorporated.

All you peoples: Excerpt from scripture is from the *New American Bible with Revised New Testament and Psalms,* Copyright © 1991, 1986, 1970 Confraterniy of Christian Doctrine, Inc., Washington, DC. Used with permission. All rights reserved. No portion of the *New American Bible* may be reprinted without permission in writing from the copyright holder.

Distant and: In *Favorite Poems of Henry Wadsworth Longfellow,* Doubleday & Company, Inc.

They began: From *Another Country,* Dell Publishing, 1962. Copyright © 1960, 1962, by James Baldwin.

Then the: From *Traveling Mercies* by Anne Lamott, copyright © 1999 by Anne Lamott. Used by permission of Pantheon Books, a division of Random House, Inc.

O Come: From Byzantine Saturday Vespers, Tone IV translated by J. Michael Thompson.

Let us: "Anthem" by W. H. Auden in *The New Oxford Book of Christian Verse* edited by Donald Davie, Oxford University Press, 1981, originally published in *Collected Poems* by W. H. Auden, Faber and Faber Ltd.

I myself: In *Music in Early Christian Literature* edited by James McKinnon, © Cambridge University Press 1987. Reprinted with the permission of Cambridge University Press.

In the: In *Music in Early Christian Literature* edited by James McKinnon, © Cambridge University Press 1987. Reprinted with the permission of Cambridge University Press.

In considering: From *Dies Domini.*

The gospel: From *Gospel Light,* Crossroad Publishing Company, copyright © 1998 by John Shea.

Much Gesture: Reprinted by permission of the publishers and the Trustees of Amherst College from *The Poems of Emily Dickinson,* Thomas H. Johnson, ed., Cambridge Mass.: The Belknap Press of Harvard University Press, Copyright © 1951, 1955, 1979 by the President and Fellows of Harvard College.

All Scripture: In *Music in Early Christian Literature* edited by James McKinnon, © Cambridge University Press 1987. Reprinted with the permission of Cambridge University Press.

Come, let: "Come, Let Us Gather" by Madeleine L'Engle in *The Weather of the Heart, poems by Madeleine L'Engle,* Harold Shaw Publishers, 1978. Copyright © Crosswicks, 1978.

You probably: From *Cathedral* by Raymond Carver, copyright © 1983 by Raymond Carver. Used by permission of Alfred A. Knopf, a division of Random House, Inc. For United Kingdom: "A Small Good Thing" Reprinted by permission of International Creative Management, Inc. Copyright © 1981 by Raymond Carver, 1989 by Tess Gallagher.

On the: In *The Faith of the Early Fathers,* Volume One, selected and translated by W. A. Jurgens, © 1970 The Liturgical Press, Collegeville, Minnesota. Used with permission.

A lamb: From *The Eucharist and the Hunger of the World* by Monica Hellwig, Paulist Press, www.paulistspress.com.

The paschal: From *Spirituality Rooted in Liturgy* by Shawn Madigan, © 1988 The Pastoral Press.

The eucharist: From *Eucharist and Eschatology* by Geoffrey Wainwright, copyright © 1971 by Geoffrey Wainright. Used by permission of Oxford University Press, Inc. Outside of the U.S.: © 1971 Geoffrey Wainwright. Used by permission of Methodist Publishing House.

I saw: "A General Communion" by Alice Meynell in *The New Oxford Book of Christian Verse* edited by

Donald Davie, Oxford University Press, 1981. Used with permission.

At this: Excerpt from *Our Communion, Our Peace, Our Promise: Pastoral Letter on the Liturgy* by Joseph Cardinal Bernardin, Archbishop of Chicago. Copyright © 1984, Archdiocese of Chicago. Liturgy Training Publications.

The day: *The Wellspring of Worship* translated by Matthew J. O'Connell, Paulist Press, 1988.

Abba Poemen: From *The Sayings of the Desert Fathers,* translated by Benedicta Ward, SLG, Cistercian Fathers Series: Number 59. Published by Cistercian Publications, Kalamazoo, Michigan, 1975.

And now: From *For the Life of the World,* 1973. Reprinted with permission of St. Vladimir's Seminary Press.

Once the: From *Dies Domini.*

At Our Lady: From *Gather Faithfully Together, Guide for Sunday Mass,* Archdiocese of Chicago: Liturgy Training Publications, 1997.

The first: Text: Thomas H. Troeger (born 1945) From *Borrowed Light* © 1994 Oxford University Press, Inc. Used by permission. All rights reserved. Photocopying this copyright material is *illegal.*

O quanta: From *The Penguin Book of Latin Verse with Plain Prose Translations of Each Poem* introduced and edited by Frederick Brittain. (Penguin Books, 1962). Copyright © by Frederick Brittain, 1962.

Sunday is: From "Day of the Lord, Day of the Church" in *Saving Signs, Wondrous Words,* copyright © 1996 Archdiocese of Chicago: Liturgy Training Publications.

Oo Oo: "Come Sunday," by Duke Ellington, 1966, © 1966 renewed G. Schirmer, Inc.

Life without: From "The Christian Week" by Peter Mazar in *At That Time.*

This is: "This Is the Day When Light Was First Created." Words: Fred Kaan. © 1968 Hope Publishing Company, Carol Stream, IL 60188. All rights reserved. Used by permission.

Thus we: From *On the Holy Spirit* excerpted and translated in *Liturgical Practice in the Fathers* by Thomas K. Carroll and Thomas Halton. Copyright © 1988 by Michael Glazier, Inc., The Liturgical Press, Collegeville, Minnesota. Used with permission.

He also: From *The Life of Constantine* quoted & translated from *Patrologia Graeca* 20:1165 in *Liturgical Practice in the Fathers* by Thomas K. Carroll and Thomas Halton. Copyright © 1988 by

Michael Glazier, Inc., The Liturgical Press, Collegeville, Minnesota. Used with permission.

Christ, having: From Byzantine Saturday Vespers, Tone VI translated by J. Michael Thompson.

As the: From *The Lord's Day* by Paul K. Jewett. William B. Eerdmans Publishing Company. Used by permission of Fuller Theological Seminary.

Only on: From "The Christian Week" by Peter Mazar in *At That Time.*

Spirit of: From the Foundling Hospital Collection, 1774, alt.

The bishop: Excerpt from the English translation of *Ceremonial of Bishops* © 1989, International Committee on English in the Liturgy, Inc. All rights reserved.

Now what: From *The Eucharistic Prayer and the Meaning of Sunday* by J. A. Jungmann, SJ, Notre Dame, IN: Fides Publishers, Inc.

The Day: Translated in *Liturgical Practice in the Fathers* by Thomas K. Carroll and Thomas Halton. Copyright © 1988 by Michael Glazier, Inc., The Liturgical Press, Collegeville, Minnesota. Used with permission.

The martyrs: From *The Church at Prayer,* Volume IV of *The Liturgy and Time* translated by Matthew J. O'Connell, published by The Liturgical Press, copyright © 1986 by The Order of St. Benedict, Inc., Collegeville, Minnesota. All rights reserved. Used with permission.

Sunday is: From *Code of Canon Law,* New English Translation. This translation, foreword, and index © copyright 1998 by Canon Law Society of America. Used with permission.

This is: "Sunday Psalm" from *Times Three* by Phyllis McGinley, copyright 1932–1960 by Phyllis McGinley; Copyright 1938–42, 1944, 1945, 1958, 1959 by The Curtis Publishing Co. Used by permission of Viking Penguin, a division of Penguin Group (USA) Inc.

Christ crucified: From Byzantine Sunday Matins, Tone I, translated by J. Michael Thompson.

We celebrate: From *Patriologia Latina* 20, 555 quoted and translated in *Dies Domini.*

Out in: "Easter Monday" by Christina Rossetti in *The New Oxford Book of Christian Verse* chosen and edited by Donald Davie. Oxford University Press, 1981. Used with permission.

And on: In *Liturgical Practice in the Fathers* by Thomas K. Carroll and Thomas Halton. Copyright © 1988 by Michael Glazier, Inc., The Liturgical Press, Collegeville, Minnesota. Used with permission.

Praise: From *The Book of Common Prayer of the Antiochian Syrian Church* translated into English by Bede Griffiths, John XXIII Center, Fordham University.

Sunday is: From *In Die Dominica Paschae* II, 52: *Corpus Christianorum Series Latina* 78, 550 translated in *Dies Domini*.

Into creation's: Translated from the Greek by John Mason Neale (1818–1866), altered.

What hard: From *The Timbered Choir, Sabbath Poems 1979–1997*, copyright 1998 by Wendell Berry. Reprinted by permission of his publisher. All rights reserved.

Today Christ: From Byzantine Sunday Divine Liturgy, Tone VIII, translated by J. Michael Thompson.

Let him: From "Wreck of the Deutschland" by Gerard Manley Hopkins in *A Hopkins Reader* by John Pick, published by Image Books, 1966, copyright © 1953, 1966 by Oxford University Press.

The prophets: From "Liturgy and Justice: An Intrinsic Relationship" in *Living No Longer for Ourselves: Liturgy and Justice in the Nineties* edited by Kathleen Hughes, RSCJ, and Mark R. Francis, CSV. Copyright © 1991 by The Order of St. Benedict, Inc., Collegeville, Minnesota. All rights reserved. Used with permission.

Christ is: From *Patrologia Graeca* 12:751 translated in *Liturgical Practice in the Fathers* by Thomas K. Carroll and Thomas Halton. Copyright © 1988 by Michael Glazier, Inc., The Liturgical Press, Collegeville, Minnesota. Used with permission.

The word: From "The Congregation and Injustice Rectified" by Romano Guardini in *Preparing Yourself for Mass*. English translation copyright © 1993, Sophia Institute.

Liturgy and: From "Serving the Lord with Justice" by Mark Searle in *Sunday Morning: A Time for Worship* edited by Mark Searle, published by The Liturgical Press, 1982. Used with permission of the Notre Dame Center for Liturgy.

Sabbath is: Reproduced from *Proclaim Jubilee!* by Maria Harris. Used by permission of Westminster John Knox Press.

Peacemaking: From "World Peace: Eucharistic Challenge" by Carol Frances Jegen, BVM, in *Chicago Studies* 19 (Summer 1980, Number 2). Copyright © 1980 Civitas Dei Foundation.

It would: From "Sunday Rest: A Contemplative Approach to Worship" by Benedicta Boland, OSB, in *Sunday Morning: A Time for Worship* edited by Mark Searle, published by The Liturgical Press, 1982. Used with permission of the Notre Dame Center for Liturgy.

Sunday Afternoon

The Sabbath: From *Sabbath* by Wayne Muller, copyright © 1999 by Wayne Muller. Used by permission of Bantam Books, a division of Random House, Inc.

The command: From "Holy Leisure and the Sabbath Tradition" in *Liturgy* 8 (1987), © 1987 The Liturgical Conference, Inc. All rights reserved. Used by permission.

Good Sabbaths: From *Sabbath Sense* by Donna Schaper, copyright © 1997 Donna Schaper. Used by permission of Augsburg Fortress (www.augsburg fortress.org).

No man: From *The Decline of Pleasure* by Walter Kerr, Simon and Schuster, 1962. Used by permission of Christopher Kerr.

The Sabbath: From "Creation and Freedom in the Celebration of the Sabbath" in *Major Feasts and Seasons* 2 (1977), © 1977 The Liturgical Conference, Inc. All rights reserved. Used by permission.

Oh, look: From "Catching My Grandson" in *Blessings the Body Gave* by Walt McDonald. Ohio State University Press, copyright © 1998 by Walter McDonald. Used by permission of the author.

Every Sunday: "The Nursing Home on a Sunday Afternoon," from *The Cloister Walk* by Kathleen Norris, copyright © 1996 by Kathleen Norris. Used by permission of Riverhead Books, an imprint of Penguin Group (USA) Inc.

What I: Excerpt from *Surprised by Joy: the Shape of My Early Life* by C. S. Lewis, copyright © 1956 by C. S. Lewis and renewed 1984 by Arthur Owen Barfield, reprinted by permission of Harcourt, Inc.

Families and: Selection from *Family* by Herbert Gold. Reprinted with the permission of Herbert Gold. Copyright © 1981 by Herbert Gold.

Della and: Excerpt from *The Long Loneliness* by Dorothy Day. Illustrated by Fritz Elchenberg. Copyright 1952 by Harper & Row, Publishers, Inc.; renewed © 1980 by Tamar Teresa Hennessy. Reprinted by permission of HarperCollins Publishers Inc.

This time: Excerpts from page 129 from *The Intimate Merton: His Life from His Journals* by Thomas Merton and edited by Patrick Hart and Jonathan Montaldo. Copyright © 1999 by the Merton Legacy Trust. Reprinted by permission of HarperCollins Publishers Inc.

There was: From *Pigeon Feathers and Other Stories* by John Updike, copyright © 1962 and renewed 1990 by John Updike. Used by permission of Alfred A. Knopf, a division of Random House, Inc. For

United Kingdom and Commonwealth excluding Canada: from "Packed Dirt, Churchgoing, A Dying Cat, A Traded Car" from *Pigeon Feathers and Other Stories* by John Updike, (Penguin, 1965). Copyright © John Updike, 1965. Reproduced by permission of Penguin Books, Ltd.

Today I: From *Dies Domini.*

Some old: From *The Sayings of the Desert Fathers,* translated by Benedicta Ward, SLG, Cistercian Fathers Series: Number 59. Published by Cistercian Publications, Kalamazoo, MI, 1975.

It will: From "Sunday—Being Made Whole in the Company of Others" in *Liturgy* 20 (April 1975), © 1975 The Liturgical Conference, Inc. All rights reserved. Used by permission.

Come, let: From *The Mennonite Hymnal.* © 1969 Herald Press: Scottdale, PA 15683. Used by permission.

At first: From "Day of the Lord, Day of the Church" in *Saving Signs, Wondrous Words,* copyright © 1996 Archdiocese of Chicago: Liturgy Training Publications.

The sad: From "The Christian Week" by Peter Mazaar in *At That Time.*

The angel: From *The Service of the Sunday Orthros,* translated by N. Michael Vaporis. Brookline, Massachusetts: Holy Cross Orthodox Press, copyright © 1991, 1994 by Nomikos Michael Vaporis. Reprinted by permission of Holy Cross Orthodox Press.

Sunday is: From "The Role of Sunday in American Society: Has it Changed?" by William C. McCready in *Sunday Morning: A Time for Worship* edited by Mark Searle, published by The Liturgical Press, 1982. Used with permission of the Notre Dame Center for Liturgy.

It is: From *Patrologia Latina* 72.18 excerpted and translated in *Liturgical Practice in the Fathers* by Thomas K. Carroll and Thomas Halton. Copyright © 1988 by Michael Glazier, Inc., The Liturgical Press, Collegeville, Minnesota. Used with permission.

The God: From *Sabbath* by Wayne Muller, copyright © 1999 by Wayne Muller. Used by permission of Bantam Books, a division of Random House, Inc.

As the: In *Practicing Our Faith* edited by Dorothy C. Bass, copyright © 1997 by Jossey-Bass, Inc., Publishers. This material is used by permission of John Wiley & Sons, Inc.

What stood: Poem from *The Timbered Choir, Sabbath Poems 1979–1997,* copyright 1998 by Wendell Berry. Reprinted by permission of his publisher. All rights reserved.

On the: Excerpt from Hillary of Poitiers (Treatise on Psalm 91, nos. 3, 4–5, 7: *Patrologia Latina* 9, 495–98; from a series of French readings, *Lectures chrétiennes pour notre temps,* published by the Abbaye d'Orval in Belgium; all rights reserved), English translation is reproduced with permission from *Christian Readings: Volume II: 17th Sunday of the Year to Advent, Year II,* copyright © 1972 Catholic Book Publishing Co., NY. All rights reserved.

It would: From *Dies Domini.*

Now resting: From *Paradise Lost* by John Milton in *The Poetical Works of John Milton* edited by David Masson. New York: Macmillan and Co., 1890.

In the: From *Sabbath* by Wayne Muller, copyright © 1999 by Wayne Muller. Used by permission of Bantam Books, a division of Random House, Inc.

But you: Excerpt, pp. 112–13 from *The Prayers of St. Augustine* by Barry Ulanov. Copyright © 1983 by Barry Ulanov. Reprinted by permission of Harper-Collins Inc.

My ego: From *Deep Is the Hunger* by Howard Thurman. Friends United Press, 1979. Used by permission.

Ceasing labor: Reproduced from *Proclaim Jubilee!* by Maria Harris. Used by permission of Westminster John Knox Press.

The Loon: "The Loon on Oak-Head Pond" by Mary Oliver from *House of Light* by Mary Oliver. Copyright © 1990 by Mary Oliver. Reprinted by permission of Beacon Press, Boston.

Obviously, the: Excerpts from *The Sabbath: Its Meaning for Modern Man* by Abraham Joshua Heschel. Copyright © 1951 by Abraham Joshua Heschel. Copyright renewed 1979 by Sylvia Heschel.

Consider the: "Camas Lilies" from *Blessing the Bread: Meditations* by Lynn Ungar. Boston: Unitarian Universalist Association, 1995.

Stopping by: From *Sabbath Time* by Tilden Edwards, The Seabury Press, 1982.

It would: From *The Decline of Pleasure* by Walter Kerr, Simon and Schuster, 1962. Used by permission of Christopher Kerr.

Sometimes, when: From *Sabbath* by Wayne Muller, copyright © 1999 by Wayne Muller. Used by permission of Bantam Books, a division of Random House, Inc.

By indirections: From *Hamlet* in *The Works of Shakespeare* edited by Edward Dowden. London: Methuen & Co. Ltd. Used by permission of Thomson Publishing Services.

After the: From *Keeping the Sabbath Wholly* by Marva J. Dawn. Copyright © 1989 by William B.

Eerdmans Publishing Co. All rights reserved. Used by permission of the publisher.

To eat: Excerpt from pages 52–53 from *Wishful Thinking: A Theological ABC* by Frederick Buechner. Copyright © 1973 by Frederick Buechner. Reprinted by permission of HarperCollins Publishers Inc.

Ibi sunt: From *The Penguin Book of Latin Verse with Plain Prose Translations of Each Poem* introduced and edited by Frederick Brittain (Penguin Books, 1962). Copyright © Frederick Brittain, 1962.

The Church: From *Bed and Board* by Robert Farrar Capon. Simon and Schuster, 1965.

Some hae: In *The Communion of Saints, Prayers of the Famous,* edited by Horton Davies. William B. Eerdmans Publishing Company, 1990.

Eight a.m.: "My Daily Bread" by Ron Hansen in *America,* March 18, 2000. Copyright 2000. All rights reserved. Reprinted with permission of America Press. For subscription information, visit www.americamagazine.org.

The table: From *The Humanity of Man* by Edmond Barbotin translated by Matthew J. O'Connell. Copyright © 1975, Orbis Books, Maryknoll, N.Y. 10545. Used by permission of the publisher.

Buber recounts: Copyright 1986 Christian Century. Reprinted with permission from the March 5, 1986 issue of the *Christian Century.*

Blessed are: Excerpt from *A Book of Blessings,* Copyright © Concacan Inc., 1981. All rights reserved. Used with permission of the Canadian Conference of Catholic Bishops.

Chicken is: From *Much Depends on Dinner* by Margaret Visser. Collier Books, Macmillan Publishing Company, 1986.

Sundays and: "Sunday Supper" from *Come Sunday* written by Nikki Grimes; Illustrated by Michael Bryant. Copyright 1996. Published by Eerdmans Publishing Company. (800) 253-7521, www.eerdmans.com/youngreaders. Used by permission, all rights reserved.

You can't: "Sundays" from *Angel to Angel: A Mother's Gift of Love* by Walter Dean Myers. Copyright © 1998 by Walter Dean Myers. Used by permission of HarperCollins Publishers.

You shall: From *Das fliessende Licht der Gottheit* quoted and translated by Mary Jeremy Finnegan, OP in *The Women of Helfta, Scholars and Mystics.* Copyright © 1991 by The University of Georgia Press.

Jesus . . . tells: From "Blessed by God for Food and Feast" in *Liturgy, Journal of the Liturgical Conference* 15 (No. 2) © 1999 by the Liturgical Conference, Inc. All rights reserved. Used by permission.

Be present: In *The Communion of Saints, Prayers of the Famous,* edited by Horton Davies. William B. Eerdmans Publishing Company, 1990.

Exodus 16: From "Preaching and Practicing Sabbath and Jubilee" by Marie Dennis in *Rite* (February/March 2000) Archdiocese of Chicago, Liturgy Training Publications.

There is: In *Simply Living, the Spirit of the Indigenous People* edited by Shirley Ann Jones, published by New World Library. Copyright © 1999 by Shirley Ann Jones. Used by permission of the publisher.

I said: Note from *The Timbered Choir, Sabbath Poems 1979–1997,* copyright 1998 by Wendell Berry. Reprinted by permission of his publisher. All rights reserved.

The gesture: "If You Have Nothing" from *The Selected Poetry of Jessica Powers* published by ICS Publications, Washington, DC. All copyrights, Carmelite Monastery, Pewaukee WI. Used with permission.

Find a: "How to Own Land" from *Saludos! Poemas de Nuevo Mexico: Poems of New Mexico,* selected and edited by Jeanie C. Williams and Victor di Suvero; translations edited by Consuelo Luz. Tesuque, NM: Pennywhilstle Press, 1995. Used by permission of New World Library.

Look, it: In *Simply Living, the Spirit of the Indigenous People* edited by Shirley Ann Jones, published by New World Library. Copyright © 1999 by Shirley Ann Jones. Used by permission of the publisher.

What is: From *Sabbath Sense* by Donna Schaper, copyright © 1997 Donna Schaper. Used by permission of Augsburg Fortress (www.augsburgfortress.org).

Jesus of: From *A New Zealand Prayer Book.* San Francisco: HarperCollins, 1997.

What an: From *Mary Barton, A Tale of Manchester Life,* by Elizabeth Gaskell, edited with an introduction by Stephen Gill. Penguin Books, 1970.

A Catholic: From "Times of Yearning, Practices of Faith" by Craig Kykstra and Dorothy C. Bass in *Practicing Our Faith* edited by Dorothy C. Bass, copyright © 1997 by Jossey-Bass, Inc., Publishers. This material is used by permission of John Wiley & Sons, Inc.

Lord, give: "The White Meat" by Jean Nordhaus in *The Other Side of the Hill, 1975–1995.* Forest Woods Media Productions, Inc., 1986. The poem first appeared in *West Branch.*

The supper: From "Day by Day" by Dorothy Day in *The Catholic Worker,* March 1934. Used with permission.

To offer: From *Hospitality to the Stranger* by Thomas Ogletree, Westminster John Knox Press, 2003. Used by permission of the author.

Sabbath is: From *Sabbath* by Wayne Muller, copyright © 1999 by Wayne Muller. Used by permission of Bantam Books, a division of Random House, Inc.

In the: From "Hospitality" by Ana María Pineda in *Practicing Our Faith* edited by Dorothy C. Bass, copyright © 1997 by Jossey-Bass, Inc., Publishers. This material is used by permission of John Wiley & Sons, Inc.

A classic: From *Sabbath Time* by Tilden Edwards, The Seabury Press, 1982.

One day: From "Commentary Column" by Dorothy Day. *The Catholic Worker,* January 1934, 3. Used with permission.

One of: From "The Christian Week" by Peter Mazar in *At That Time.*

Now, tell: From *Seven Gothic Tales* by Isak Dinesen, copyright 1934 by Harrison Smith & Robert Hass, Inc. and renewed 1962 by Isak Dinesen. Used by permission of Random House, Inc.

When we: From *Keeping the Sabbath Wholly* by Marva J. Dawn. Copyright © 1989 by William B. Eerdmans Publishing Co. All rights reserved. Used by permission of the publisher.

He is: Verse of a hymn by Ann Griffiths translated from Welsh by H. A. Hodges in *Songs to Her God* by A. M. Allchin, Cowley Publications, Boston, 1987.

In Exodus: From *Sabbath* by Wayne Muller, copyright © 1999 by Wayne Muller. Used by permission of Bantam Books, a division of Random House, Inc.

Has anything: "A Country Road" by Sanford Lyne in *Louisiana Literature* 16 (Fall 1999).

We sat: Excerpt from *My Antonia* by Willa Cather (Boston: Houghton Mifflin, 1995). Used by permission of the publisher.

The grip: Excerpts from page 129 from *The Intimate Merton: His Life from His Journals* by Thomas Merton and edited by Patrick Hart and Jonathan Montaldo. Copyright © 1999 by the Merton Legacy Trust. Reprinted by permission of HarperCollins Publishers Inc.

The fume: Poem from *The Timbered Choir, Sabbath Poems 1979–1997,* copyright 1998 by Wendell Berry. Reprinted by permission of his publisher. All rights reserved.

Sunday Night

However we: From *Sabbath Time* by Tilden Edwards, The Seabury Press, 1982.

Someone holds: From *A Book of Family Prayer* by Gabe Huck. New York: The Seabury Press, 1979.

At vanishing: "Epicenter of Joy" by Catherine de Vinck in *God of a Thousand Names* published by Alleluia Press. Copyright Catherine de Vinck, 1993, Allendale, NJ 07401.

Presently we: Excerpt from *My Antonia* by Willa Cather (Boston: Houghton Mifflin, 1995). Used by permission of the publisher.

Trinity of: Translated by J. M. Neale in *Songs of Syon* edited by Reverend G. R. Woodward. London: Schott & Company, 1923.

Never was: From "Evening" by Stephen Lubega in *Poems from East Africa* edited by David Cook & David Rubadiri. Nairobi: Heinemann, 1990.

In the: From The *Stanbrook Abbey Hymnal,* © Stanbrook Abbey 1974.

While the: From *The Service of the Sunday Orthros,* translated by N. Michael Vaporis. Brookline, Massachusetts: Holy Cross Orthodox Press, copyright © 1991, 1994 by Nomikos Michael Vaporis. Reprinted by permission of Holy Cross Orthodox Press.

The evening: From *Mary Barton, A Tale of Manchester Life,* by Elizabeth Gaskell, edited with an introduction by Stephen Gill. Penguin Books, 1970.

He who: From "Eternity" by William Blake in *A Book of Religious Verse* edited by Helen Gardner. New York: Oxford University Press, 1972.

We resign: From *Prayers Written at Vailima* by Robert Lewis Stevenson. London: Chatto & Windus, 1910.

We must: From *The Decline of Pleasure* by Walter Kerr, Simon and Schuster, 1962. Used by permission of Christopher Kerr.

They walked: Excerpt from "The Wide Net" from *The Wide Net and Other Stories,* copyright 1942 renewed 1970 by Eudora Welty, reprinted by permission of Harcourt, Inc.

Music ingathers: "The Evening Chimes" by Jessica Powers from *Selected Poetry of Jessica Powers* edited by Regina Siegfried, ASC, and Robert F. Morneau, ICS Publications, Washington, DC. All copyrights, Carmelite Monastery, Pewaukee, Wisconsin. Used with permission.

Cold dark: Excerpt from "At the Fishhouses" from *The Complete Poems 1927–1979* by Elizabeth Bishop. Copyright © 1979, 1983 by Alice Helen Mothfessel. Reprinted by permission of Farrar, Straus and Giroux, LLC.

As a day: From *Dies Domini.*

And thus: From *For the Life of the World* by Alexander Schmemann. St. Vladimir's Seminary Press, 1973. Used by permission of St. Vladimir's Seminary Press.

Meanwhile the: From *The Weight of Glory and Other Addresses* by C. S. Lewis. William B. Eerdmans, 1966.

The father: From "The Glass and the Bowl" from *Baptism of Desire* by Louise Erdrich. Copyright © 1990 by Louise Erdrich. Reprinted by permission of HarperCollins Publishers Inc.

The hare: From "Twilight Calm" by Christina Rossetti in *The Complete Poems of Christina Rossetti,* volume I, edited by R. W. Crump. Copyright © 1979 by Louisiana State University Press.

What if: Reprinted by permission of Louisiana State University Press from *Out in the Open: Poems* by Margaret Gibson. Copyright © 1989 by Margaret Gibson.

Postlude—Monday

Sunday is: From "On Celebrating Sunday" by Urban T. Holmes in *Liturgy* 20 (April 1975), © 1975 The Liturgical Conference, Inc. All rights reserved. Used by permission.

Blaze of: From "Monday Lauds," Office Hymn texts by Fr. Aelred Squire, OSB CAM, © 1994 Camaldolese Hermits of America.

When we: From "Times of Yearning, Practices of Faith" by Craig Dykstra and Dorothy C. Bass in *Practicing Our Faith* edited by Dorothy C. Bass, copyright © 1997 by Jossey-Bass, Inc., Publishers. This material is used by permission of John Wiley & Sons, Inc.

Whatever is: Poem from *The Timbered Choir, Sabbath Poems 1979–1997,* copyright 1998 by Wendell Berry. Reprinted by permission of his publisher. All rights reserved.

When the: From *The Service of the Sunday Orthros,* translated by N. Michael Vaporis. Brookline, Massachusetts: Holy Cross Orthodox Press, copyright © 1991, 1994 by Nomikos Michael Vaporis. Reprinted by permission of Holy Cross Orthodox Press.

God created: From *Roots, Deep and Strong* by Mary E. Penrose, OSB, New York: Paulist Press, 1995, www.paulistpress.com.

It is: From *Concerning the City of God Against the Pagans* by Saint Augustine, translated by Henry Bettenson. (Penguin Books, 1972). Translation © Henry Bettenson, 1972.

Take pleasure: From *Radical Optimism, Rooting Ourselves in Reality* by Beatrice Bruteau. New York: Crossroad Publishing Company, 1993.

Abba Poeman: From *The Sayings of the Desert Fathers,* translated by Benedicta Ward, SLG, Cistercian Fathers Series: Number 59. Published by Cistercian Publications, Kalamazoo, MI, 1975.

My work: From *Living Out Loud* by Anna Quindlen, copyright © 1987 by Anna Quindlen. Used by permission of Random House, Inc. United Kingdom and British Commonwealth: Reprinted by permission of International Creative Management, Inc. Copyright © 1987.

All this: Excerpt from "Welcome Morning," from *The Awful Rowing Toward God* by Anne Sexton. Coyright © 1975 by Loring Conant, Jr., Executor of the Estate of Anne Sexton. Reprinted by permission of Houghton Mifflin Company. All rights reserved.

The Sabbath: Excerpt from *The Sabbath: Its Meaning for Modern Man* by Abraham Joshua Heschel. Copyright © 1951 by Abraham Joshua Heschel. Copyright renewed by Sylvia Heschel.

These coppers: From *Shadows on the Rock* by Willa Cather, copyright 1931 by Willa Cather and renewed 1959 by the Executors of the Estate of Willa Cather. Used by permission of Alfred A. Knopf, a division of Random House, Inc.

Each person: From *The Work Trap* by Martin C. Helldorfer. Mystic, Connecticut: Twenty-Third Publications, 1995.

As the: From *For the Life of the World* by Alexander Schmemann. St. Vladimir's Seminary Press, 1973. Used by permission of St. Vladimir's Seminary Press.

The late: Excerpt from The *Quotidian Mysteries* by Kathleen Norris. Copyright © 1998 by Kathleen Norris. Paulist Press, Inc, New York/Mahwah, NJ. Used with permission of Paulist Press. www.paulist press.com.

Notes

Notes

Notes

DATE DUE

HIGHSMITH 45230